HOLIDAY STORYBOOK STEW

COOKING THROUGH THE YEAR WITH BOOKS KIDS LOVE

SUZANNE I. BARCHERS

PETER J. RAUEN

ILLUSTRATED BY

DARCIE CLARK FROHARDT

fulcrum resources

GOLDEN, COLORADO

Copyright © 1998 Suzanne I. Barchers and Peter J. Rauen
Cover and interior illustrations copyright © 1998 Darcie Clark Frohardt
Book design by Deborah Rich

Library of Congress Cataloging-in-Publication Data
Barchers, Suzanne I.
    Holiday storybook stew : cooking through the year with books kids
    love / Suzanne I. Barchers, Peter J. Rauen ; illustrated by Darcie Clark
    Frohardt.
        p.   cm.
    Includes bibliographical references and index.
    ISBN 1-55591-972-3 (pbk.)
    1. Holiday cookery—Juvenile literature.   2. Holidays—Juvenile
literature.   3. Handicraft—Juvenile literature.   4. Children's stories,
American.   I. Rauen, Peter J.   II. Title.
TX739.B323   1998
641.5'68—dc21   98-14700
                                                                CIP

Printed in the United States of America
0 9 8 7 6 5 4 3 2 1

Fulcrum Publishing
16100 Table Mountain Parkway, Suite 300
Golden, Colorado 80401-5093
(800) 992-2908 • (303) 277-1623
website: www.fulcrum-resources.com
e-mail: fulcrum@fulcrum-resources.com

CONTENTS

CHAPTER 4: APRIL 29

CHAPTER 5: MAY 37

CHAPTER 6: JUNE 49

CHAPTER 7: JULY 57

CHAPTER 8: AUGUST 61

INTRODUCTION

Nothing tastes better than a hot dog on the Fourth of July, cider on Halloween, or turkey on Thanksgiving. Good food has become such an integral part of holidays that many family gatherings focus on the preparation and consumption of these memorable feasts.

Holiday Storybook Stew: Cooking Through the Year with Books Kids Love combines three favorite pastimes: reading great books, exploring related activities, and cooking. Beginning with Martin Luther King, Jr. Day and ending with New Year's Eve, the thirty-five featured books relate to a holiday or observation. Note that holidays whose observations vary, such as Easter, occur in the month they first might appear.

Each featured book is summarized, followed by a related activity, experiment, or art project. A brief booklist provides additional stories that can serve as a supplement or replacement to the featured book. Finally, after reading the featured book, readers can enjoy preparing a recipe inspired by the story and holiday. Each recipe lists tools needed, ingredients, and detailed steps for easy preparation.

Most of the recipes in this book have been developed to provide a traditional amount of food for a family of four to six. Teachers or group leaders who use these recipes may want to double or triple them or make several items for a tasting party. Be certain that none of the children have medical, cultural, or religious reasons to avoid certain foods.

Some recipes have more steps than others or may require the use of knives, an oven, or the stove. Adults who are just beginning to work with children should select recipes appropriate for the children's ages and adapt them or assign tasks accordingly.

Once you have mastered a few recipes, create an entire meal of favorites. Try these sample menus, adding beverages where needed:

BREAKFAST

Mother's Fruit Kabobs with Yogurt Dip
George's Corn Cakes

LUNCH

Good Neighbor Potato Soup
Thanksgiving Pumpkin Muffins
Chocolate Soda

DINNER

Bacon-Wrapped Dates
Victory Garden Stuffed Peppers
Groundhog's Zucchini Bread
Tantrum Fudgies

PICNIC

Picnic Cheese Spread
The Best Hot Dogs
Trail Mix Bites

After you have prepared a recipe, take time to note any changes you need to make for the next time. Altitude adjustments are given in Appendix A. See Appendix B for measuring tips and equivalents. Additional children's books on food are included in the Bibliography. Read the following cooking and safety tips with your child before beginning to cook. And remember to have fun! *Bon appétit!*

COOKING TIPS

1   Read entire recipe before beginning.

2   All temperatures are in Fahrenheit.

3   All-purpose white flour should be used unless otherwise noted. When pepper is called for, use black pepper unless otherwise noted.

4   Look up unknown cooking terms in the Glossary on page 111 or in the dictionary.

5   Gather all tools together before starting: utensils, bowls, and other equipment.

6   Gather all ingredients.

7   Check and adjust position of oven racks before turning on oven.

8   Turn on the oven to preheat when appropriate.

9   Measure exactly.

10   Complete each step before going on to the next one.

11   Carefully time any baking or cooking. Use a kitchen timer, if possible, or a clock that is easy to read.

12   To check baked goods for doneness, insert a toothpick. If the toothpick comes out sticky, return the item to the oven for a few more minutes.

13   To melt butter, microwave on high for ten or more seconds in a glass container or melt on stove over low heat in a small saucepan.

SAFETY TIPS

1   Ask for an adult's help when using the oven or stove. Always use thick and dry potholders to handle hot equipment.

2   Turn off stove and oven when cooking and baking are done.

3 If grease should catch fire, pour baking soda on the fire. Do not pour water over the flames. If the fire is in a pan, put the lid on to smother the flames. Do not turn on a fan to remove smoke until you are sure the fire is fully extinguished.

4 Tie back long or loose hair when using an electric mixer, stove, or oven. Remove jewelry. Avoid loose sleeves or clothing. Wear an apron to protect clothes from spills.

5 Keep hands and face away from steam when cooking on the stove.

6 Turn the saucepan handles to the inside.

7 Keep sharp tools on tables when not in use.

8 Move the blade away from your hands when using a vegetable peeler.

9 Use a cutting board when cutting or chopping ingredients. Always cut away from your hands.

10 Have adults help wash knives and other sharp tools. Wipe blades carefully.

11 Use dry hands when plugging in electrical appliances.

12 Do not immerse electrical appliances in water when cleaning them. Refer to manufacturer's directions for cleaning.

13 Wash hands before handling food.

CHAPTER 1

JANUARY

Martin Luther King, Jr. Day

(third Monday)

OUR MARTIN LUTHER KING BOOK

by Patricia C. McKissack
(Chicago: Children's Press, 1986)

Mrs. Stevens explains to the class who Martin Luther King, Jr. was and why it is important to celebrate his birthday. The students role-play how difficult segregation can be, make books about Dr. King, and send cards to the Martin Luther King, Jr. Center in Atlanta, Georgia. At a birthday party, they celebrate with southern punch and by beginning a freedom garden.

FREEDOM GARDEN

MATERIALS:

Styrofoam cups
Planting soil
Seeds for red, white, and blue
    flowers, such as pansies
Markers

DIRECTIONS:

Fill the Styrofoam cups one-half to three-quarters full with soil. Plant two or three seeds in each cup. Mark the cup with the color of the flower. Water carefully and place in appropriate lighting, away from extreme temperatures. Save the seed packets for later use. When spring comes, decide on a pleasing arrangement for the flowers by drawing a color pattern on paper. Plant the flowers using the designated distances from the seed packets. Water and tend the garden carefully and enjoy the display all summer long.

RELATED BOOKS

Jones, Kathryn. *Happy Birthday, Dr. King!* New York: Simon and Schuster, 1994.
McDonnell, Janet. *Martin Luther King Day.* Chicago: Children's Press, 1993.
Sorenson, Lynda. *Martin Luther King, Jr. Day.* Vero Beach, Fla.: Rourke Press, 1994.

RASPBERRY AND ORANGE SHERBET PUNCH

TOOLS:

Measuring cups
Measuring spoon
Blender

4 10-ounce glasses
Spoons

INGREDIENTS:

2 cups frozen raspberries
$^3/_4$ cup cold water
1 tablespoon lemon juice
2 tablespoons honey

$^1/_4$ cup sugar
1 cup orange sherbet
4 sprigs fresh mint

STEPS: SERVES 4

1   Place the raspberries into the blender. Add the water, lemon juice,
    honey, and sugar. Holding onto the top of the blender, mix on high for
    1 to 2 minutes until the raspberries are blended.

2   Pour 6 ounces of the raspberry mixture into each glass.

3   Place $^1/_4$ cup of orange sherbet into each glass.

4   Garnish the top of each glass with a fresh mint sprig and eat with a
    spoon.

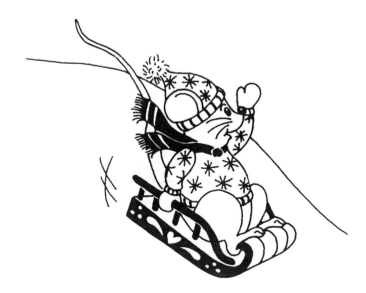

NOTES

CHAPTER 2

FEBRUARY

GROUNDHOG DAY (FEBRUARY 2)

A GARDEN FOR A GROUNDHOG

by Lorna Balian
(NASHVILLE, TENN.: ABINGDON PRESS, 1985)

On Groundhog Day the groundhog sees that the O'Learyses' garden isn't planted yet and goes back to bed. Once springtime arrives, the O'Learys plan a special area for the groundhog so he won't disturb their garden, but they discover that groundhogs don't read!

OUTDOOR FEEDERS

MATERIALS:

Suet
Heavy saucepan
Bird seed
Pinecones
Waxed paper
Stale bagels
Yarn
Tree, bush, or fence

DIRECTIONS:

Help feed birds and other outdoor creatures during this cold month by creating a variety of items to hang from a tree, bush, or fence. Obtain suet from the butcher. Heat it in a saucepan until it starts to melt. Role the pine cones in the suet and then in the bird seed. Let cool on waxed paper. Tie stale bagels with yarn and tie to the tree, bush, or fence. Repeat with the pine cones.

RELATED BOOKS

Gerstein, Mordicai. *Daisy's Garden.* New York: Hyperion Books, 1995.
Glass, Marvin. *What Happened Today, Freddy Groundhog?* New York: Crown Publishers, 1989.
Kroll, Steven. *It's Groundhog Day!* New York: Holiday House, 1987.
Warren, Jean. *Huff and Puff on Groundhog Day.* Everett, Wash.: Warren Publishing, 1995.

GROUNDHOG'S ZUCCHINI BREAD

TOOLS:

2 mixing bowls
Measuring cups
Measuring spoons
Wooden spoon
Fork
Paper towel

Cutting board
Knife
Grater
Pastry brush
2 $8\frac{1}{2}$ x $4\frac{1}{2}$ loaf pans

INGREDIENTS:

3 cups flour
$1\frac{1}{4}$ cup sugar
$4\frac{1}{2}$ teaspoons baking powder
1 teaspoon salt
4 eggs

$\frac{2}{3}$ cup vegetable oil
6 small zucchini
$\frac{1}{2}$ teaspoon lemon extract
1 tablespoon vegetable oil

STEPS: MAKES 2 LOAVES

1   Place the flour, sugar, baking powder, and salt in a mixing bowl. Mix with the wooden spoon.

2   Crack the eggs into the other mixing bowl. Add vegetable oil. Beat mixture with the fork.

3   Rinse the zucchini under cold water. Place on a paper towel to dry.

4   Place the zucchini on the cutting board. Cut off and discard the ends.

5   Grate the zucchini into the mixing bowl with the eggs and oil. (You may use a food processor instead of a grater.) Add the lemon extract.

6   Mix with the wooden spoon.

7   Pour the zucchini mixture into the flour mixture. Mix with the wooden spoon until well blended.

8   Lightly grease the loaf pans with the pastry brush and 1 tablespoon vegetable oil. Divide the batter between the two loaf pans.

9   Bake in a preheated 350°F oven for 60 minutes. Cool 10 minutes before removing from pans. Let cool on a rack before slicing.

Note: You may want to add 1 cup chopped nuts to the flour mixture.

VALENTINE'S DAY (FEBRUARY 14)

HEART TO HEART

by George Shannon
(BOSTON: HOUGHTON MIFFLIN, 1995)

Squirrel is dismayed when he realizes he has forgotten Valentine's Day and that Mole is coming with a Valentine's cake. Squirrel dashes about his den, gathering together materials to make a valentine. In the process he remembers a variety of events they've enjoyed together, incorporating them, and making the best valentine ever.

VALENTINE MEMORY BOX

MATERIALS:

Various mementos—Postcard, Ribbon, Stone, Photograph, Drawing, Souvenir, Small toy, Plastic ring, Dried flowers
Shoe box or other small box
Tissue paper
Materials for decorating the box

DIRECTIONS:

Collect a variety of mementos that will remind the recipient of your memory box of special times together. Place in the box with the tissue paper. Decorate the box with construction paper hearts, paint, and so forth.

RELATED BOOKS

Barkin, Carol. *Happy Valentine's Day!* New York: Lothrop, Lee and Shepard Books, 1988.

Brown, Marc. *Arthur's Valentine.* Boston: Little, Brown, 1980.

Kroll, Steven. *Will You Be My Valentine?* New York: Holiday House, 1993.

Modell, Frank. *One Zillion Valentines.* New York: Trumpet Club, 1981.

VALENTINE COOKIES

TOOLS:

Measuring cups
Large mixing bowl
Electric mixer
Wooden spoon
Plastic wrap
Rolling pin

Heart shaped cookie cutter, 2 inches in
    diameter
Cookie sheet
Measuring spoon
Fork
Small mixing bowl
Pastry brush

INGREDIENTS:

1 cup butter, softened
8 ounces cream cheese, softened
$2\frac{1}{4}$ cups flour

$\frac{1}{2}$ cup raspberry jam
2 eggs
2 tablespoons milk
$\frac{1}{4}$ cup powdered sugar

STEPS: MAKES 16 COOKIES

1 Place the softened butter and cream cheese in a large mixing bowl.

2 Beat with the electric mixer for 2 minutes on medium.

3 Slowly blend in the flour with the wooden spoon.

4 Place the dough on a clean dry surface. Knead until smooth.

5 Wrap the dough in plastic wrap. Refrigerate for 2 hours.

6 Remove dough and place on a clean, dry surface. Roll out the dough
   into a rectangle that is $\frac{1}{8}$ inch thick.

7 Using the cookie cutter, cut out 32 hearts. Place 16 hearts onto the
   cookie sheet. Set the others aside.

8 Place $\frac{1}{2}$ tablespoon raspberry jam into the centers of the 16 hearts.

9 Cover each heart with the remaining 16 hearts. Gently press down the
   edges with the fork.

10 Break the eggs into a small mixing bowl. Add the milk. Beat for 30
    seconds with the fork.

11 Use the pastry brush and lightly brush the tops of the hearts with the
    egg mixture.

12 Place the hearts into a preheated 400°F oven for 10 to 12 minutes or
    until lightly browned.

13 Remove the cookies from the oven and cool for 10 minutes. Sprinkle
    with powdered sugar.

9

PRESIDENTS' DAY (THIRD MONDAY)

GEORGE WASHINGTON'S BREAKFAST

by Jean Fritz
(NEW YORK: COWARD MCCANN, 1969)

George W. Allen, born on February 22, wonders what George Washington had for breakfast. He checks at the library and goes to a museum but can't find out exactly what Washington liked. Finally he finds an old book written by a contemporary of Washington who shares that he liked three Indian hoecakes a day. Soon George is enjoying three hoecakes, just like Washington.

CORN AND SALT MODELING DOUGH

MATERIALS:

Measuring cups
Saucepan
1 cup cornstarch
1 cup salt
$\frac{1}{2}$ cup boiling water
Tempera paint

DIRECTIONS:

Mix cornstarch, salt, and boiling water in the saucepan. Stir until mixture is very stiff. Remove from heat and let cool. Knead cooled dough. Mixture can be used as a modeling clay, dried, and painted with tempera paint.

RELATED BOOKS

d'Aulaire, Ingri Mortenson. *Abraham Lincoln.* New York: Doubleday, 1939.

Harness, Cheryl. *Young Abe Lincoln: The Frontier Days, 1809–1837.* Washington, D.C.: National Geographic Society, 1996.

Sorenson, Lynda. *Presidents Day.* Vero Beach, Fla.: Rourke Press, 1994.

Tunnell, Michael O. *The Joke's on George.* New York: William Morrow, 1993.

10

GEORGE'S CORN CAKES

TOOLS:

Medium bowl
Fork
Measuring cups
Measuring spoon

Wooden spoon
Griddle
Spatula

INGREDIENTS:

1 egg
2 cups cornmeal
$^3/_4$ teaspoon salt
$1^1/_2$ cups milk

Grease for griddle
Butter
Powdered sugar or syrup

STEPS: MAKES 10–12

1 Crack egg into bowl. Beat with fork.

2 Stir in cornmeal, salt, and milk with the wooden spoon.

3 Drop spoonfuls of batter on a well greased, hot griddle.

4 Fry until brown on both sides, turning with the spatula.

5 Serve hot with butter, powdered sugar, or syrup.

(Adapted from *Cooking Up U.S. History: Recipes and Research to Share with Children*, by Suzanne I. Barchers and Patricia C. Marden. Englewood, Colo.: Teacher Ideas Press, 1991, p. 24.)

International Friendship Month

JALAPEÑO BAGELS

by Natasha Wing
(New York: Atheneum, 1996)

Pablo can't decide what to do for International Day at school. His mother prepares food from her Mexican heritage, and his father's bagels and challah are also delicious. Finally he decides to make jalapeño bagels, representing the blending of his Mexican and Jewish backgrounds. Use the recipes in the back of the book or try the following recipe.

FRIENDSHIP MOSAIC

MATERIALS:

Egg cartons
Colored paper scraps or confetti
Scissors
Glue or paste
Tweezers or large needle
Construction paper or tagboard

DIRECTIONS:

Use confetti, magazine pictures, or paper scraps for small pieces of paper. Cut paper as necessary and sort colors into an egg carton. Think of a mosaic that blends colors, just as Pablo's family blended their backgrounds. Experiment with a variety of arrangements until a pleasing pattern emerges. Lift each piece, apply paste, and replace. Leave space between each piece if you wish.

RELATED BOOKS

Carle, Eric. *Do You Want to Be My Friend?* New York: Crowell, 1971.
Dale, Penny. *Daisy Rabbit's Tree House.* Cambridge, Mass.: Candlewick Press, 1995.
Lies, Brian. *Hamlet and the Enormous Chinese Dragon Kite.* Boston: Houghton Mifflin, 1994.
McPhail, David. *Lost!* Boston: Little, Brown, 1990.

JALAPEÑO BAGELS

TOOLS:

Saucepan
Measuring cups
Measuring spoons
Thermometer
2 small bowls
1 large mixing bowl
1 large glass bowl

Wooden spoon
Pastry brush
Glass bowl
Dishcloth
4-quart saucepan
Slotted spoon
Cookie sheet

INGREDIENTS:

1 cup milk
$\frac{1}{4}$ cup vegetable oil
1 tablespoon honey
$\frac{1}{4}$ teaspoon salt
1 tablespoon dry yeast

1 egg
$2\frac{1}{2}$ cups whole wheat flour
1 cup white flour
2 tablespoons diced jalapeños
2 quarts water

EGG WASH:

1 egg yolk beaten with 1 tablespoon cold water

STEPS: MAKES 12

1 Place milk, vegetable oil, honey, and salt in a small saucepan. Heat to 90°F. Remove from heat and add the yeast.

2 Separate the white from the yolk of the egg into 2 small mixing bowls.

3 Beat the egg white until frothy. Add egg white to the milk and yeast mixture. Save the egg yolk for the egg wash.

4 Mix the whole wheat and white flours together in a large bowl.

5 Place half the flour mixture in a large mixing bowl. Make a well in the center. Pour in the milk mixture and blend with the wooden spoon.

6 Blend the diced jalapeños into the dough.

7 Add the remaining flour to the bowl. Mix together with clean, dry hands.

8 Remove the flour mixture from the bowl. Place it on a clean floured surface. Knead until the dough is smooth.

9 Using the pastry brush, lightly grease a glass bowl. Place the kneaded dough in it. Brush the top of the dough with oil. Cover the bowl with a clean, dry cloth. Let stand in a warm place for 1 hour.

10 Place the dough on a clean, dry surface. Divide dough into 4 equal parts. Roll each piece into 12-inch strips. Then cut into thirds.

11 Shape each piece into rings and press the ends together. Let stand on the board for 10 minutes.

12 Use the pastry brush to lightly grease the baking sheet.

13 Heat the 2 quarts of water in a large pan until very hot, but not boiling. Place the rolled dough into the water, 2 at a time. When the dough rises to the top, use a slotted spoon carefully to turn them over. Cook for another 2 minutes.

14 Remove the bagels with the slotted spoon and place them on the cookie sheet. When all are on the baking sheet, brush each with the egg wash. If you prefer, sprinkle sesame or poppy seeds onto the bagels now.

15 Bake in a preheated oven at 400°F for approximately 15 minutes or until golden brown.

CHAPTER 3

MARCH

CHOCOLATE WEEK (FIRST WEEK)

THE CHOCOLATE-COVERED-COOKIE TANTRUM

by Deborah Blumenthal
(NEW YORK: CLARION, 1997)

Sophie and her mother are on the way home from the park when Sophie sees another girl eating a chocolate-covered cookie. Sophie decides right then that she has to have a cookie, but it's too close to supper. This leads to a tantrum and eventual exhaustion. After a nap with her blanket, Sophie is ready for dinner—and chocolate-covered cookies.

COUNTING THE BIRDS

DIRECTIONS:

Many birds participate in this story about Sophie. After reading it, look through all the illustrations and count the number of birds who watch, get scared, or fly away. On page 19, count how many feet are kicking through the air and onto the ground. What other things can you count?

RELATED BOOKS

Alexander, Martha. *And My Mean Old Mother Will Be Angry, Blackboard Bear.* New York: Dial, 1972.

Erickson, Karen. *I Was So Mad.* New York: Viking, 1987.

Martin, Jane Read, and Patricia Marx. *Now I Will Never Leave the Dinner Table.* New York: HarperCollins, 1996.

Orozco, José Orozco. "The Chocolate." In *De Colores: and Other Latin-American Folk Songs for Children.* New York: Dutton, 1994.

Sharmat, Marjorie Weiman. *Attila the Angry.* New York: Holiday House, 1985.

TANTRUM FUDGIES

TOOLS:

2-quart saucepan
Measuring cups
Wooden spoon

Teaspoon
Waxed paper

INGREDIENTS:

2 cups sugar
$\frac{1}{4}$ cup cocoa
$\frac{1}{2}$ cup milk

1 stick butter
$\frac{1}{2}$ cup peanut butter
3 cups oatmeal

STEPS: MAKES 3–4 DOZEN

1   Place sugar, cocoa, and milk in saucepan. Cook over medium heat, stirring occasionally with the wooden spoon. Bring to boil and let boil 1 minute. Remove from heat.

2   Stir in butter, peanut butter, and oatmeal. Stir until thoroughly melted and mixed.

3   Let stand 5 minutes.

4   Use the teaspoon to drop spoonsful on the waxed paper. Cookies will become firm in 45 to 60 minutes. Store in a plastic container.

Note: This may be prepared in a microwave oven by substituting a microwave-proof mixing bowl for the saucepan.

PASSOVER
(14–22 OF NISAN ON THE JEWISH CALENDAR)

THE MATZAH THAT PAPA BROUGHT HOME

by Fran Manushkin
(NEW YORK: SCHOLASTIC, 1995)

In repetitive, cumulative verse, a young girl shares the tradition of Passover from father bringing home the matzah to the feast to the sharing of the Four Questions.

DIPPED CANDLES

MATERIALS:

Newspapers
2 1-pound coffee cans
Saucepan
1 pound paraffin
Cotton string
Fork

DIRECTIONS:

This activity requires adult supervision. Spread newspapers on table. Fill one coffee can about two-thirds full of water and place in saucepan. Fill the other can with cold water. Fill the saucepan about half full of water. Put over medium heat on stove. As the water in the saucepan begins to boil, add chunks of paraffin to the can inside the saucepan until almost full. As the wax melts, it forms a layer on top of the water. The wax needs to be just the right temperature so it won't slide off the string. If it is too cold it will be too thick for dipping. Keep the pan on low heat.

Cut a piece of string two times as long as the can. Lay the string over the prongs of a fork so that both sides hang down equally. Weave the portion that lies over the fork among the prongs to hold the string in place. Dip the string into the can until it touches the bottom. Pull the string out of the can and dip it in the can of cold water to harden. Continue dipping the string into the wax and cold water until candles are as thick as desired. Trim the wicks to about half an inch before burning candles.

(From Suzanne I. Barchers and Patricia C. Marden's *Cooking Up U.S. History: Recipes and Research to Share with Children.* Englewood, Colo.: Teacher Ideas Press, 1991.)

RELATED BOOKS

Goldin, Barbara Diamond, reteller. *The Magician's Visit: A Passover Tale.* New York: Penguin, 1993.

Wohl, Laren L. *Matzoh Mouse.* New York: HarperCollins, 1991.

Yolen, Jane. *Milk and Honey: A Year of Jewish Holidays.* New York: G. P. Putnam's Sons, 1996.

Zalben, Jane Breskin. *Happy Passover, Rosie.* New York: Henry Holt, 1990.

Note: Use with menorah on page 90.

PAPA'S MATZAH BALLS

TOOLS:

Small mixing bowl
1-quart mixing bowl
Measuring cups
Measuring spoons
Electric mixer
Rubber spatula

2-quart saucepan
Glass bowl
Slotted spoon
Plate
4-quart saucepan
Ladle

INGREDIENTS:

3 eggs
$1/_2$ cup plus 1 tablespoon matzah
    meal
1 teaspoon salt

$1/_4$ teaspoon white pepper
2 cups canned chicken broth
2 cups cold water
4 cups canned chicken broth

STEPS: SERVES 6

1 Crack the eggs, one at a time. Separate the whites from the yolks, placing the yolks into the small bowl and the whites into the 1-quart mixing bowl.

2 Using the electric mixer, beat the whites on high for 4 minutes until stiff.

3 Add the egg yolks. Continue to beat for an additional 1 minute.

4 Slowly add the matzah meal to the mixing bowl, blending with the rubber spatula.

5 Blend in the salt and white pepper with the rubber spatula. Let the mixture stand for 8 to 10 minutes.

6 Place 2 cups of chicken broth into the 2-quart saucepan. Heat on medium heat.

7 Place the cold water into the glass bowl. You will use this to dip your hands in while rolling the matzah balls.

8 Divide the matzah into 18 equal portions. Roll them into round balls.

9 Place the balls into the heated chicken broth, 1 at a time. Cook 6 at a time for 12 to 15 minutes. When they are done, remove with the slotted spoon and place on the plate.

10 When all the matzah balls are done, heat the 4 cups chicken broth in the 4-quart saucepan. Add the cooked matzah balls. Turn down the heat and simmer for 10 minutes.

11 Ladle 6 ounces of the heated broth into 6 soup bowls. Add 3 matzah balls to each bowl and serve.

21

St. Patrick's Day (March 17)

LEPRECHAUNS NEVER LIE

by Lorna Balian
(WATERTOWN, WISC.: HUMBUG BOOKS, 1980)

Gram is ailing and Ninny Nanny says she will catch a leprechaun to get some gold. Find out if she is successful and then enjoy some potato soup with this amusing story.

SHAMROCK BOUQUET

MATERIALS:

Green and brown construction paper
3 brown pipe cleaners
Glue
Approximately 8 $\frac{1}{2}$ x 11 heavy white
    paper or tagboard
Scissors

DIRECTIONS:

Fold nine 3-inch squares of the green construction paper. Using the scissors, cut the squares into heart shapes. Create a flowerpot by cutting out the brown paper in the appropriate shape. Glue the bottom half of the pot onto the tagboard. Place one of the pipe cleaners in the top part of the pot, slightly to one side. Cluster three heart shapes together at the top of the pipe cleaner to make a shamrock. When satisfied with the arrangement, glue in place. Repeat by creating the other two shamrocks, perhaps bending one pipe cleaner so that the shamrock hangs over the side. Additional shamrocks can be added as preferred. Display or use as a card.

RELATED BOOKS

Baker, James W. *St. Patrick's Day Magic.* Minneapolis, Minn.: Lerner Publications, 1990.
Barth, Edna. *Shamrocks, Harps, and Shillelaghs: The Story of the St. Patrick's Day Symbols.* New York: Clarion Books, 1977.
Bunting, Eve. *St. Patrick's Day in the Morning.* New York: Clarion Books, 1980.
Freeman, Dorothy Rhodes. *St. Patrick's Day.* Hillside, N.J.: Enslow Publishers, 1992.
Gibbons, Gail. *St. Patrick's Day.* New York: Holiday House, 1994.

GOOD NEIGHBOR POTATO SOUP

TOOLS:

Cutting board
Knife
Measuring spoons
Saucepan with lid
Wooden spoon

Vegetable peeler
1-quart mixing bowl
Blender
Measuring cup

INGREDIENTS:

1 small yellow onion
2 tablespoons butter
4 russet potatoes
2 cups water

2 teaspoons salt
1 cup whole milk
$1/2$ teaspoon white pepper

STEPS: SERVES 6–8

1   Place the onion on the cutting board. Carefully cut off and discard the ends. Slice the onion in half. Remove the skin. Cut the onion halves into $1/4$-inch cubes.

2   Place the butter in the pan. Add the onion cubes. Cook on low, stirring with the wooden spoon for 3 minutes.

3   While the onions are cooking, use the vegetable peeler to remove the skins from the potatoes. Discard skins.

4   Place the potatoes on the cutting board. Carefully cut them into $1/4$-inch cubes.

5   Place the cut potatoes into the pan with the onion. Add the water and salt. Increase heat to medium high. Bring to a boil and cook for 15 minutes.

6   Reduce heat to low. Cover pan and let simmer for 10 minutes.

7   Remove pan from heat. Spoon out half the potato mixture into the mixing bowl. Place into the refrigerator to chill for 30 minutes. Set the pan aside.

8   Remove chilled potato mixture from refrigerator and spoon into blender. Blend on high for 1 minute.

9   Add $1/4$ cup milk to the blender. Blend on medium for 30 seconds, holding down the lid. Pour the blended mixture into the pan and place on low heat.

10   Add the remaining milk and white pepper. Simmer over low heat for 20 minutes. Stir with wooden spoon every 30 seconds. Serve hot.

EASTER

(FIRST SUNDAY AFTER THE FULL MOON ON OR AFTER MARCH 21)

THE BIG BUNNY AND THE EASTER EGGS

by Steven Kroll
(NEW YORK: HOLIDAY HOUSE, 1982)

Wilbur prepares for Easter early but gets sick on Easter Eve. His friends try to deliver the eggs but fail. Finally they convince Wilbur to get out of bed so that the children can have their baskets. With the help of his friends he delivers them but has to place them in a variety of unusual places. The near disaster results into today's favorite event—the Easter Egg Hunt!

EGGHEADS

MATERIALS:

Eggshell halves
Markers
3- x 5-inch cards
Tape
Tablespoon
Potting soil
Grass seed
Water

DIRECTIONS:

Decorate an eggshell half by drawing facial features: eyes, eyebrows, nose, lips, and cheeks. To make a stand for the head, cut a 1-inch strip from the 3- x 5-inch card. Decorate it with a bow tie or a necklace. Tape the ends together. Set the egg on the stand. Use a tablespoon to gently spoon soil into the egg. Sprinkle grass seed over the soil. Water the seed. Sprinkle lightly with water every day for a week and watch your egghead's hair grow.

RELATED BOOKS

Auch, Mary Jane. *The Easter Egg Farm.* New York: Holiday House, 1992.
Barth, Edna. *Lilies, Rabbits, and Painted Eggs: The Story of the Easter Symbols.* New York: Clarion Books, 1970.
Polacco, Patricia. *Just Plain Fancy.* New York: Trumpet Club, 1990.

BUNNY'S EGG SALAD ON CRACKERS

TOOLS:

2-quart saucepan
Measuring cups
Paper towels
Cutting board
Measuring spoons

Knife
2-quart mixing bowl
Fork
Wooden spoon

INGREDIENTS:

4 eggs
4 cups water
1 tablespoon salt
$1/4$ cup plain yogurt
$1/4$ cup sour cream
$1/2$ tablespoon cider vinegar

1 tablespoon Dijon mustard
$1/2$ teaspoon salt
$1/4$ teaspoon white pepper
1 green onion
24 crackers
Parsley sprigs

STEPS: SERVES 4-6

1 Gently place the eggs in the saucepan. Add the water and salt. Place on a burner on medium-high heat. Bring water to a boil. Cook for 12 to 15 minutes.

2 Place the saucepan in a sink. Pour out the hot water. Run cold water over the eggs for 2 minutes.

3 Carefully tap the cooled eggs on the edge of the sink to crack the shell. Using clean hands, press the shell with your thumb, holding the egg in the palm of your hand. Place the egg under running water and remove the shell.

4 Place the peeled eggs on paper towels. Pat dry.

5 Place the eggs on the cutting board. Cut the eggs in half lengthwise. Then cut them into $1/4$-inch pieces.

6 Place the cut eggs into the mixing bowl. Add the yogurt, sour cream, cider vinegar, Dijon mustard, salt, and white pepper. Blend the ingredients together with the fork.

7 Place the green onion on the cutting board. Cut into $1/8$-inch pieces. Add to the egg mixture and blend with the wooden spoon.

8 Chill egg salad for at least 1 hour.

9 Spoon a tablespoon of egg salad onto 24 crackers. Place on a serving dish. Garnish with parsley sprigs.

MARDI GRAS

(SHROVE TUESDAY, THE LAST DAY OF CARNIVAL)

MARDI GRAS: A CAJUN COUNTRY CELEBRATION

by Diane Hoyt-Goldsmith
(NEW YORK: HOLIDAY HOUSE, 1995)

Joel, who lives in the bayou country of Louisiana, gives readers a detailed description in words and photographs of what Mardi Gras is like in his town. Beginning with the history of the Acadians, Joel describes why and how Mardi Gras is celebrated. Finally, readers enjoy the music, food, parades, and other festivities of the event.

PLASTER MASKS

MATERIALS:

Plaster tape
Scissors
Newspapers
Warm water
Shower cap
Vaseline
Towel
Glitter, markers, sequins, feathers
Glue
Elastic

DIRECTIONS:

This requires an adult partner. Cut plaster tape into many lengths between 3 and 6 inches long. Spread out newspapers. Prepare water. Have child tuck hair in shower cap and spread Vaseline generously all over the face, including eyebrows and hairline. Have child lie down on newspapers.

Take a longer plaster strip, dip into the water, squeeze out the water, and lay along the edges of the child's face. Continue laying the strips, smoothing them as you go. Work inward, using shorter strips for areas around the nose, lips, and eyes. Leave space below the nose for breathing. Repeat for at least two layers of plaster strips.

When plaster tingles it has begun to set. Remove when it lifts away easily. Allow to dry before punching holes in the sides for the elastic. Decorate, add elastic, and wear for Mardi Gras!

RELATED BOOK

Coil, Suzanne M. *Mardi Gras!* New York: Macmillan, 1994.

SEAFOOD GUMBO

TOOLS:

Small saucepan
Measuring cups
Spoon
Large soup pot

Knife
Measuring spoons
Serving bowls

INGREDIENTS:

$1\frac{1}{4}$ cups oil
$1\frac{1}{4}$ cups flour
$1\frac{1}{2}$ cups chopped onion
$\frac{1}{2}$ cup chopped celery
$\frac{1}{4}$ cup chopped green pepper
2 cloves garlic, chopped
2 tomatoes, peeled and chopped
3 quarts chicken broth

$\frac{1}{4}$ cup chopped parsley
$\frac{1}{2}$ teaspoon pepper
1 teaspoon salt
3 bay leaves
2 pounds small shrimp, shelled
$\frac{1}{2}$ pound crabmeat
2 dozen oysters and their juice
3 cups cooked rice

STEPS: SERVES 10

1   Heat 1 cup of the oil in small saucepan over medium heat. Add flour and stir. Cook over low heat for about 30 minutes until mixture, called "roux," is dark brown.

2   Pour $\frac{1}{4}$ cup oil into a large soup pot. Heat over medium heat. Add onion and cook until clear.

3   Add celery, green pepper, and garlic to onion. Cook 5 minutes.

4   Add roux to onion mixture and cook 10 minutes, stirring constantly.

5   Add tomatoes to mixture. Add chicken broth and turn heat to medium high. Stir well and add parsley, pepper, salt, and bay leaves.

6   Bring to a boil. Lower heat and simmer for 45 minutes.

7   Add shrimp and crabmeat. Bring to a boil. Remove from heat.

8   Chop oysters into large pieces. Add oysters and their juice to mixture and stir well. Remove bay leaves from gumbo.

9   Put rice in the bottom of each serving bowl and pour gumbo over it.

(From Suzanne I. Barchers and Patricia C. Marden's *Cooking Up U.S. History: Recipes and Research to Share with Children.* Englewood, Colo.: Teacher Ideas Press, 1991.)

NOTES

CHAPTER 4

APRIL

APRIL FOOLS' DAY (APRIL 1)

APRIL FOOLS' DAY

by Emily Kelley
(MINNEAPOLIS, MINN.: CAROLRHODA BOOKS, 1983)

No one knows exactly how April Fools' Day originated. One theory is that people in France noticed that there were more fish in the streams in April. These young fish were so easy to catch they were called poisson d'Avril, *April fish. Also, Napoleon Bonaparte married his wife on April 1 and was nicknamed* Poisson d'Avril. *Read other "fishy" theories about this day in Emily Kelley's entertaining book.*

RAINBOW MAGIC

MATERIALS:

¹/₂ cup grape juice
Large glass
1 tablespoon baking soda
¹/₂ cup water in cup
1 tablespoon vinegar
¹/₂ cup water in cup

DIRECTIONS:

Pour the grape juice in the glass. Mix the baking soda in the half cup of water. Mix the vinegar in the other half cup of water. Pour some of the baking soda mixture into the grape juice. What happens? Add some of the vinegar solution. What happens? Repeat by alternating the process. Make up some magic words to use to trick your friends.

RELATED BOOKS

Kroll, Steven. *It's April Fools' Day.* New York: Holiday House, 1990.
Modell, Frank. *Look Out, It's April Fools' Day.* New York: Greenwillow Books, 1985.
Stevenson, James. *Mud Flat April Fool.* New York: Greenwillow Books, 1998.

APRIL TUNA MELT

TOOLS:

Can opener
1-quart mixing bowl
Fork
Cutting board
Knife

Measuring cup
Measuring spoons
Wooden spoon
Baking sheet

INGREDIENTS:

1 8-ounce can of tuna
1 stalk celery
2 sprigs green onion
$1/4$ cup mayonnaise
$1/4$ cup plain yogurt

1 tablespoon Dijon mustard
1 dash Worcestershire sauce
1 teaspoon black pepper
4 slices English muffins
4 slices Swiss cheese

STEPS: MAKES 4

1   Open and drain the can of tuna. Place tuna in the mixing bowl. Use the fork to pull apart the tuna into small pieces.

2   Place the celery on the cutting board. Cut the rib in half lengthwise. Then cut into $1/8$-inch pieces. Place in mixing bowl.

3   Place the green onions on the cutting board. Cut into $1/8$-inch pieces. Place in mixing bowl.

4   Add the mayonnaise, yogurt, mustard, Worcestershire sauce, and pepper to the tuna, celery, and onion.

5   Place the English muffins on the baking sheet. Spoon equal parts of the tuna mixture onto the muffins. Top each with a slice of cheese.

6   Bake in a preheated 350°F oven for 25 minutes. Serve hot.

EARTH DAY (APRIL 22)

PEARL MOSCOWITZ'S LAST STAND

by Arthur Levine
(NEW YORK: TAMBOURINE BOOKS, 1993)

Pearl, who loves to eat noodle pudding, watches her neighborhood grow, enjoying the new cultures introduced by her new neighbors. However, she is dismayed when the city repeatedly cuts down the old flowering trees in the name of progress. When the last tree is about to be bulldozed, Pearl ensures that no one will cut down this tree.

WORM GARDEN

MATERIALS:

1 large package chocolate sandwich cookies
Plastic zipper bag
2 large boxes (7 ounces) instant chocolate pudding
1 large package whipped topping
$\frac{1}{2}$ to $\frac{2}{3}$ cup milk
Flower pots

DIRECTIONS:

Crush cookies in zipper bag or a food processor. Save approximately one fourth of the cookies. Mix the milk and instant pudding. Mix in the whipped topping and remaining cookies. Place in a flower pot. Sprinkle remaining crumbs on top. You can add a branch after wrapping its stem in foil or plastic.

RELATED BOOKS

Bunting, Eve. *Someday a Tree.* New York: Clarion Books, 1993.
Crenson, Victoria. *Bay Shore Park: The Death and Life of an Amusement Park.* New York: W. H. Freeman, 1995.
Lowery, Linda. *Earth Day.* Minneapolis, Minn.: Carolrhoda Books, 1991.
MacLachlan, Patricia. *All the Places to Love.* New York: HarperCollins, 1994.
McDonnell, Janet. *Celebrating Earth Day.* Chicago: Children's Press, 1994.

PEARL'S NOODLE PUDDING (LOKSHEN KUGEL)

TOOLS:

Measuring cups
2-quart saucepan
Wooden spoon
Large mixing bowl
Measuring spoons
Electric mixer

Cutting board
Knife
Small saucepan
Pastry brush
1-quart casserole dish

INGREDIENTS:

2 cups milk
$1/4$ pound dry spaghetti noodles
3 eggs
$1/2$ teaspoon vanilla extract
1 tablespoon lemon juice
$1/3$ cup sugar

$1/4$ teaspoon salt
$1/2$ teaspoon cinnamon
$1/4$ teaspoon nutmeg
$1/2$ cup dried apricots
$1/2$ cup raisins
3 tablespoons butter, melted

STEPS: SERVES 6–8

1 Heat the milk in the 2-quart saucepan over medium high. When the milk begins to boil, add the spaghetti. Stir with a wooden spoon every 30 seconds or so for 12 to 15 minutes until the noodles are soft.

2 Set the noodles aside to cool in the milk for a half hour.

3 In the large mixing bowl, crack the eggs. Add the vanilla, lemon juice, sugar, salt, cinnamon, and nutmeg. Mix with the electric mixer on low for 1 minute.

4 Cut the dried apricots on the cutting board into $1/4$-inch pieces.

5 Add the apricots and raisins to the egg mixture.

6 Add 2 tablespoons of the butter to the egg mixture.

7 Pour the cooled noodles and milk into the egg mixture. Stir with the wooden spoon.

8 Using the pastry brush, grease the casserole dish with the remaining tablespoon of butter.

9 Carefully pour the egg and noodles into the casserole dish and place into a preheated 350°F oven. Bake for 45 minutes. Carefully insert a knife into the center of the casserole. If it comes out clean, the pudding is done.

Arbor Day (last Friday)

PEARL PLANTS A TREE

by Jane Breskin Zalben
(New York: Simon and Schuster, 1995)

Grandpa shows Pearl the apple tree he planted many years ago, and she decides to plant a tree too. After carefully planting a seed, she waits through the long winter, dreaming of when the tree will be big. Finally spring arrives and her seedling is big enough to plant outside.

EXPLORING SEEDS

MATERIALS:

Large, old wool socks
Tweezers
Microscope or magnifying glass

DIRECTIONS:

Put the wool socks on over your shoes and walk through a vacant lot or woods. Your socks will collect a variety of seeds. Use the tweezers to pick them off later. Examine them using a microscope or magnifying glass. Repeat this every month or so and compare the kinds of seeds that you collect throughout the changing seasons.

RELATED BOOKS

Bunting, Eve. *Someday a Tree.* New York: Clarion Books, 1993.

Burns, Diane L. *Arbor Day.* Minneapolis, Minn.: Carolrhoda Books, 1989.

Ikeda, Daisaku. *The Cherry Tree.* New York: Alfred A. Knopf, 1991.

Lerner, Harriet, and Susan Goldhor. *What's So Terrible About Swallowing an Apple Seed?* New York: HarperCollins, 1996.

Locker, Thomas. *Sky Tree.* New York: HarperCollins, 1995.

Stevens, Jan Romero. *Carlos and the Squash Plant.* Flagstaff, Ariz.: Northland Publishing, 1993.

34

APPLE WALNUT SALAD

TOOLS:

Dish cloth
Cutting board
Knife
Glass bowl
Strainer
Mixing bowl

Wooden spoon
Measuring cups
Measuring spoons
Wire whip
Wooden spoon
Plastic wrap

INGREDIENTS:

6 red delicious apples
1 lemon
$\frac{1}{2}$ cup plain yogurt
$\frac{1}{4}$ cup sour cream

3 tablespoons brown sugar
$\frac{1}{2}$ teaspoon vanilla extract
$\frac{1}{2}$ tablespoon cinnamon
$\frac{1}{2}$ cup walnuts

STEPS: SERVES 8–10

1   Wash the apples under cool water. Dry with a clean cloth.

2   Place the apples on the cutting board one at a time. Carefully cut in half. Cut each piece again.

3   Cut out and discard seeds from the center.

4   Cut all apple pieces lengthwise into fourths. Place pieces in the glass bowl.

5   Carefully cut the lemon in half. Hold the strainer over the glass bowl. Squeeze the lemon over the apples in the bowl. Toss apples with the wooden spoon and set aside.

6   Place the yogurt, sour cream, sugar, vanilla, and cinnamon in a mixing bowl. Blend with the wire whip for 1 minute.

7   Pour the yogurt mixture onto the apples. Toss with the wooden spoon until well coated.

8   Top the apples with the chopped walnuts. Cover the bowl with plastic wrap and refrigerate for at least 2 hours.

Note: You may add raisins, mandarin oranges, coconut flakes, or grapes to this salad.

NOTES

CHAPTER 5

MAY

MAY DAY (MAY 1)

QUEEN OF THE MAY

by Steven Kroll
(NEW YORK: HOLIDAY HOUSE, 1993)

Sylvie lives with her stepmother and stepsister. Sylvie had to do all the chores, even on holidays. On May Day she hurried to finish early so she could bring the most beautiful bouquet to the celebration and become Queen of the May. In kindness, she helps several animals while collecting the flowers, and she is captured by the hag who wants the stepsister to be queen. But the animals come to her rescue, and she enjoys the festivities as the queen.

MAY DAY BASKETS

MATERIALS:

Small plastic baskets
Potting soil
Flower seeds

DIRECTIONS:

Begin this at least a month before May Day. Fill the basket about half full with potting soil. Carefully plant the flower seeds. Water them lightly and place where they will receive appropriate light and temperature. Tend to them carefully as they grow. A traditional May Day practice is to leave the basket as a surprise on somebody's porch, ringing the doorbell and running away before being discovered. If your seeds have not begun to flower in time, add a few fresh flowers from bulbs or early spring flowers.

RELATED BOOKS

Gerstein, Mordicai. *The Story of May.* New York: HarperCollins, 1993.
Mariana. *Miss Flora McFlimsey's May Day.* New York: Lothrop, Lee and Shepard Books, 1969.

MAY DAY SALAD

TOOLS:

Cutting board
Knife
Mixing bowl
Vegetable peeler or brush
Measuring cups

Medium mixing bowl
Paper towels
4 small salad bowls
Sprigs of mint or dandelion leaves,
 optional

INGREDIENTS:

2 apples
1 large carrot
1 cup raisins

$\frac{1}{3}$ to $\frac{1}{2}$ cup mayonnaise
Lettuce leaves

STEPS: SERVES 4

1 Slice the apples in half on the cutting board. Slice them again. Remove the seeds. Cut into cubes. Place in mixing bowl.

2 Peel the skin off the carrot or scrub and rinse it. Carefully cut off and discard the ends. Cut the carrot in half lengthwise. Cut in half again. Cut into cubes. Place in mixing bowl.

3 Place raisins in mixing bowl. Add mayonnaise and mix well.

4 Wash enough lettuce leaves to line the salad bowls. Pat dry with paper towels.

5 Line the salad bowls with the leaves.

6 Arrange the salad mixture on top of the lettuce leaves.

7 Decorate with the mint or dandelion leaves to look like a spring salad.

Cinco de Mayo (May 5)

FIESTA! CINCO DE MAYO

by June Behrens
(Chicago: Children's Press, 1978)

In easy text the author describes the history behind Cinco de Mayo *and the traditions surrounding its celebration.*

THE TORTILLA FACTORY

by Gary Paulsen
(San Diego: Harcourt Brace and Company, 1995)

Loving hands plant the corn that grows into lush plants. The dried corn is used in the tortilla factory. More hands prepare the dough that goes by truck to kitchens where still more hands use the tortillas to nourish those who continue to plant the corn.

PIÑATAS

MATERIALS:

Balloon
String
Newspapers, whole and cut into
  1-inch strips
Bowl
Liquid starch
Candy and small toys
Glue
Colored tissue paper
Stick

DIRECTIONS:

Blow up a balloon and tie a string at the top. Spread out newspapers to protect the table. Pour liquid starch into a bowl. Dip strips of newspaper in liquid starch and wrap the balloon completely with only one layer of strips. Let balloon dry thoroughly.

Cut open a small plug in the piñata and fill with candy and small toys. Return plug and glue in place. Cut tissue paper into strips. Begin gluing at the bottom so the strips hang from

40

the bottom of the balloon. Add strips to the top, creating a decorative pattern. Be sure to cover the plug.

To break the piñata, hang it from a tree branch. Each player can try to hit it with a stick while blindfolded. (Be sure that adults supervise this activity.)

RELATED BOOKS

Ancona, George. *The Piñata Maker.* San Diego: Harcourt Brace, 1994.

Stevens, Jan Romero. *Carlos and the Corn Plant.* Flagstaff, Ariz.: Northland Publishing, 1995.

Vigil, Angel. *The Corn Woman: Stories and Legends of the Hispanic Southwest.* (La Mujer del Maíz: Cuentos y Leyendas del Sudoeste Hispano.) Englewood, Colo.: Libraries Unlimited, 1994.

FIESTA TORTILLAS

TOOLS:

Measuring cups
Measuring spoons
Large mixing bowl
Wooden spoon

Plastic wrap
Rolling pin
Griddle
Metal spatula

INGREDIENTS:

2 cups corn flour (*masa harina*)
1 teaspoon salt

$1\frac{1}{4}$ cups warm water (80 to 90°F)
1 tablespoon fresh lime juice

STEPS: MAKES 10

1   Place the corn flour and salt in the mixing bowl. Mix with the wooden spoon.

2   Slowly add 1 cup warm water, mixing with the wooden spoon.

3   Mix in the lime juice.

4   Using clean hands, knead the dough in the bowl, adding the remaining water 1 tablespoon at a time. When all the water is added, form dough into a ball. Set aside for 30 minutes.

5   Divide the dough into 10 equal portions. Roll each portion into a small ball.

6   Place each dough ball between 2 sheets of plastic wrap. Press down with your hands to flatten each ball. Use the rolling pin to roll each ball into a thin circle, approximately 6 inches in diameter.

7   Preheat the griddle to medium-high heat, approximately 400°F. Remove the plastic from the tortillas. Carefully place the tortillas on the griddle one at a time. Cook for 45 to 50 seconds on each side, turning with a metal spatula. If the tortillas get too dark, turn down the heat on the griddle.

MOTHER'S DAY (SECOND SUNDAY)

MOTHER'S MOTHER'S DAY

by Lorna Balian
(WATERTOWN, WISC.: HUMBUG BOOKS, 1987)

Hazel, a young mouse, takes a bouquet of violets to her mother's home, only to discover that Hazel's mom has taken a gift to her *mother. Six generations search for and finally find each other, just escaping the cat. An alternative story is* The Mother's Day Mice *by Eve Bunting (below).*

MOTHER'S DAY SACHETS

MATERIALS:

2 tablespoons whole cloves
$\frac{1}{4}$ cup dried rose petals or other dried flowers
2 tablespoons mint leaves
Few drops of rose oil or other flower oil (purchase in bath shops)
Bowl
Spoon
8-inch squares of lace or netting
12-inch ribbon

DIRECTIONS:

Mix all ingredients except the oil drops. Toss. Add the oil and toss again. Place one-eighth of the mixture in center of square. Gather the edges and tie with the ribbon. Repeat.

RELATED BOOKS

Bunting, Eve. *The Mother's Day Mice.* New York: Clarion Books, 1986.
Kroll, Steven. *Happy Mother's Day.* New York: Holiday House, 1985.
Neitzel, Shirley. *We're Making Breakfast for Mother.* New York: Greenwillow, 1997.
Sharmat, Marjorie Weinman. *Hooray for Mother's Day!* New York: Holiday House, 1986.
Wynot, Jillian. *The Mother's Day Sandwich.* New York: Orchard Books, 1990.

MOTHER'S FRUIT KABOBS WITH YOGURT DIP

TOOLS:

Paper towels
Knife

Cutting board
Big spoon

INGREDIENTS:

18 fresh strawberries
1 whole cantaloupe
1 whole honeydew melon

1 whole pineapple
6 10- to 12-inch skewers

STEPS: MAKES 6

1 Wash strawberries. Remove stems. Let dry on paper towels.

2 Using the knife and a cutting board, cut fruit in half. Then cut off ends. Clean out seeds.

3 Place canteloupe and honeydew melon on board and use a knife to cut off the skin, carefully working from the top down.

4 Cut melons into 1-inch squares.

5 Cut ends off pineapple. Place pineapple upright on cutting board. Use knife to cut off the skin, working from the top down.

6 Cut the pineapple into quarters lengthwise. Then cut into 1-inch squares.

7 Place a skewer through the center of a strawberry. Then add 1 piece of cantaloupe, 1 piece of pineapple, and 1 piece of honeydew melon. Repeat with a strawberry, cantaloupe, pineapple, and melon. Finish with 1 strawberry.

8 Serve with yogurt dip.

YOGURT DIP FOR FRUIT KABOBS

TOOLS:

Measuring cup
Measuring spoons
Blender

Serving bowl
Knife

INGREDIENTS:

6 fresh strawberries
1 cup plain yogurt

3 tablespoons honey
1 teaspoon cinnamon

STEPS:

1 Wash strawberries. Remove stems.

2 Place strawberries, yogurt, honey, and cinnamon in blender.

3 Blend on low speed for 30 seconds and pour into serving bowl.

4 Slice 2 remaining strawberries. Place on top of dip to decorate.

MEMORIAL DAY (LAST MONDAY)

MEMORIAL DAY

by Geoffrey Scott
(MINNEAPOLIS, MINN.: CAROLRHODA BOOKS, 1983)

After the Civil War, many people felt that something should be done to honor all who had died in the war. Decoration Day was celebrated on May 30 by the Grand Army of the Republic. The people marched in parades, listened to veterans, decorated graves, and ate dinners of ham, turkey, and baked beans. In 1971 President Nixon declared Memorial Day a national holiday, a time to remember those who lost their lives in war.

MARCHING STICKS

MATERIALS:

2 1-inch-thick dowels, cut into 12-inch lengths
Sandpaper
Red, white, and blue markers
Marching music

DIRECTIONS:

Sand the ends of the dowels until they are smooth. Wipe until they are dust free. Decorate with markers in red, white, and blue. Put on some marching music and march while playing the rhythm sticks.

RELATED BOOK

Sorenson, Lynda. *Memorial Day.* Vero Beach, Fla.: Rourke Press, 1994.

PICNIC BAKED BEANS

TOOLS:

Strainer
4-quart stock pot with lid
Measuring cups
Cutting board
Knife

Measuring spoons
Wooden spoon
4-quart casserole dish
Aluminum foil

INGREDIENTS:

1 pound navy beans
$1\frac{1}{2}$ quarts cold water
1 yellow onion
1 tablespoon apple cider vinegar
$1\frac{1}{2}$ tablespoons Dijon mustard

2 tablespoons brown sugar
$\frac{1}{3}$ cup dark molasses
$3\frac{1}{2}$ cups cold water
3 strips bacon

STEPS: SERVES 8–10

1   Place the beans in the strainer. Rinse under cold water. Place in the stock pot.

2   Pour the water into the pot with the beans. Place on a burner over medium-high heat and cook for 30 minutes, uncovered.

3   Remove beans from heat. Place the lid on the pot and let sit for 30 minutes.

4   Place the onion on the cutting board. Cut off and discard the ends. Cut the onion in half. Remove and discard the skin.

5   Cut the onion into $\frac{1}{3}$-inch cubes and set aside.

6   Carefully drain off the water from the beans, leaving the beans in the pot.

7   Add the cut onions, vinegar, mustard, brown sugar, and molasses to the beans. Stir well with the wooden spoon.

8   Add the $3\frac{1}{2}$ cups cold water to the beans. Carefully spoon mixture into the casserole. Top with the bacon.

9   Cover with aluminum foil.

10 Bake in a preheated 325°F oven for 2 hours.

11 Carefully remove the foil. Increase the temperature to 400°F for 10 minutes. Serve hot.

NOTES

CHAPTER 6

JUNE

FLAG DAY (JUNE 14)

THE FLAG WE LOVE

by Pam Ryan
(WATERTOWN, MASS.: CHARLESBRIDGE PUBLISHING, 1996)

Rhyming verses and beautiful illustrations describe the history of our country's flag. Sidebars provide further information regarding the importance of our flag for daily and momentous occasions. Celebrate Flag Day by making a flag and snacking on Trail Mix Bites.

FLAG MAKING

MATERIALS:

Paper
Pencil
Foil
Warming tray
Fabric, cut to desired flag size
Crayons
Paper towel
Dowel

DIRECTIONS:

This project requires an adult. Use paper and pencil to create the design for your flag. If working on a large piece of fabric, divide the fabric into appropriate grids approximately the size of the surface of the warming tray. Cover warming tray with foil. Set warming tray on low.

If your project has a pattern that can be reversed, draw directly on the foil. Hold the crayon near the end for safety. You can also place a hot pad under your hand as you work. The crayon will melt while you draw. When your drawing is done, press fabric onto the foil to absorb the crayon. Remove and let dry. Clean foil with a paper towel before doing next section.

If your project has a pattern that cannot be reversed, tape the fabric to the warming tray. Draw directly on the fabric, letting the crayon melt as it warms. Remove and let dry. Repeat as necessary.

Attach flag to dowel and display.

RELATED BOOKS

Caudill, Rebecca. *Did You Carry the Flag Today, Charley?* New York: Henry Holt, 1966.

Crampton, William. *Flag.* London: Dorling Kindersley, 1989.

Wallner, Alexandra. *Betsy Ross.* New York: Holiday House, 1994.

TRAIL MIX BITES

TOOLS:

Measuring cups
Measuring spoons
4-quart mixing bowl
Electric mixer

Rubber spatula
Wooden spoon
Pastry brush
2 cookie sheets

INGREDIENTS:

$2\frac{1}{4}$ cups flour
1 cup sugar
$\frac{1}{2}$ cup butter, softened
$\frac{1}{3}$ cup apple juice
$2\frac{1}{2}$ teaspoons baking powder
$\frac{1}{2}$ teaspoon cinnamon
$\frac{1}{2}$ teaspoon baking soda

$\frac{1}{2}$ teaspoon salt
1 egg
1 cup granola cereal
$\frac{1}{2}$ cup raisins
$\frac{1}{3}$ cup sliced almonds
$\frac{1}{2}$ cup quick-cooking oats
2 tablespoons vegetable oil

STEPS: MAKES APPROXIMATELY 32

1 Place the flour, sugar, butter, apple juice, baking powder, cinnamon, baking soda, salt, and egg into the mixing bowl.

2 Using the electric mixer, blend all the ingredients on low for 2 minutes. Stop mixer every 30 seconds and scrape the sides of the bowl with the rubber spatula.

3 Place the granola cereal, raisins, almonds, and quick-cooking oats into the mixing bowl. Blend with the wooden spoon for 1 minute.

4 Using the pastry brush, lightly grease the cookie sheets with the vegetable oil.

5 Drop tablespoons of cookie dough onto the cookie sheet about 2 inches apart. Use the back of the spoon to gently smooth out the top of each dropped cookie.

6 Bake in a preheated 350°F oven for 15 to 20 minutes.

FATHER'S DAY (THIRD SUNDAY)

HAPPY FATHER'S DAY

by Steven Kroll
(NEW YORK: HOLIDAY HOUSE, 1988)

Father's Day begins with Dad's favorite breakfast: juice, fruit and yogurt, a roll, and coffee. All the family members then share the surprises they have prepared, such as completing the chores Dad usually does. The perfect day continues with a trip to see the Green Sox play and then enjoying a pizza.

TURN-WHEEL FATHER'S DAY CARD

MATERIALS:

Assorted construction paper
Round lid
Pencil
Scissors
Brass fastener

DIRECTIONS:

Fold a 12- x 18-inch piece of construction paper so that it is 12 x 9 inches. Open it up. On the right side, use the lid to draw a half circle in the top half of the page. Cut out the half circle. Use the same lid to draw a full circle on another piece of paper. Cut it out. Use one-fourth to one-sixth of the circle to draw four to six things that you like about your father. Use the brass fastener to attach the wheel so that it can be turned. Decorate the card and write a message to your father.

RELATED BOOKS

Bunting, Eve. *A Perfect Father's Day.* New York: Clarion Books, 1991.
Mandrell, Louise, and Ace Collins. *Best Man for the Job: A Story About the Meaning of Father's Day.* Fort Worth, Tex.: The Summit Group, 1993.
Sharmat, Marjorie Weiman. *Hooray for Father's Day!* New York: Holiday House, 1987.

SWEET ROLLS

TOOLS:

Measuring cups
Small saucepan
Wooden spoon
Measuring spoons
Thermometer
Mixing bowl
Saucepan
Clean dish cloth
Pastry brush

Small glass bowl
Electric mixer
Rubber spatula
2-quart casserole dish
Rolling pin
Knife
Cooling rack
Serving dish

INGREDIENTS:

$^3/_4$ cup milk
$^1/_2$ cup sugar
1 teaspoon salt
$^1/_4$ cup water
2 eggs, beaten
2 packages dry yeast
4 cups flour

$^1/_3$ cup melted butter
1 tablespoon ground cinnamon
4 tablespoons sugar
2 tablespoons cooking oil
$^1/_3$ cup butter, softened
$^1/_2$ cup brown sugar
4 tablespoons sugar
1 tablespoon ground cinnamon

STEPS: SERVES 6-8

1   Heat milk in small saucepan on medium-high heat until it comes to a boil. Remove and stir in the $^1/_2$ cup sugar and salt. Let cool.

2   Heat the water to approximately 90°F. Place in a small glass bowl and add the yeast. Let stand for 10 minutes.

3   When the milk mixture has cooled to 90°F, add the water and yeast. Stir well. Add eggs. Mix together.

4   Place 2 cups of flour into a mixing bowl. Pour in the milk mixture and stir with the wooden spoon.

5   Melt $^1/_3$ cup butter in saucepan and pour into flour and milk mixture. Blend well with the wooden spoon. Add the cinnamon and remaining flour. Mix well with clean hands.

6   Cover the dough with a clean dish cloth. Let sit for 10 minutes.

7   Place the dough on a clean dry surface. Knead for 8 to 10 minutes.

8   Using a pastry brush, grease a glass bowl. Place the kneaded dough in it. Cover with a clean dish cloth and set aside in a warm place for $1^1/_2$ hours.

9   Place $^1/_3$ cup butter and brown sugar in a mixing bowl. Blend with an electric mixer. With a rubber spatula spread the butter and brown sugar mixture on the bottom of a 2-quart casserole. Set aside.

10   When the dough has risen, place it on a clean, floured surface.

11   Roll the dough with a rolling pin into a rectangle, twice as long as it is wide and approximately $^1/_4$ inch thick. Mix the 4 tablespoons sugar and 1 tablespoon ground cinnamon. Sprinkle the dough with the cinnamon sugar and roll like a jelly roll. Cut the roll into $1^1/_2$-inch sections and place in the casserole dish. Let the rolls stand for 10 minutes.

12   Place the rolls in a preheated 375°F oven for 20 minutes. Cool on a rack for 10 minutes.

13   Carefully place a serving dish that is slightly larger than the casserole dish upside down on the casserole dish. Using hot pads, turn it over very carefully. The top of the rolls will be covered with the butter and brown sugar.

Note: If preferred, add chopped nuts to the casserole dish after coating the bottom with the butter and brown sugar mixture.

NOTES

CHAPTER 7

JULY

INDEPENDENCE DAY (JULY 4)

MY FIRST FOURTH OF JULY BOOK

by Harriet W. Hodgson
(CHICAGO: CHILDREN'S PRESS, 1987)

Easy poems and colorful illustrations celebrate every aspect of this exciting holiday. Beginning with a birthday poem, youngsters will also enjoy poems such as "Bicycle Parade," "Skinny Sparkler," and "Hot Dog on a Stick."

FOURTH OF JULY CENTERPIECE

MATERIALS:

Newspapers
6-inch Styrofoam half circle
Glitter
Glue
Package of small flags

DIRECTIONS:

Cover your work area with newspapers. Place the Styrofoam on the papers. Cover with glue and sprinkle glitter on to cover. Let dry. Place small flags in the Styrofoam in a pleasing arrangement. If they loosen and fall out, replace with a bit of glue.

RELATED BOOKS

Anderson, Joan. *The Glorious Fourth at Prairietown.* New York: William Morrow, 1986.
Corwin, Judith Hoffman. *Patriotic Fun.* New York: Simon and Schuster, 1985.
Mandrell, Louise, and Ace Collins. *Sunrise Over the Harbor: A Story About the Meaning of Independence Day.* Fort Worth, Tex.: The Summit Group, 1993.
Schachtman, Tom. *America's Birthday: The Fourth of July.* New York: Macmillan, 1986.
Sorenson, Lynda. *Fourth of July.* Vero Beach, Fla.: Rourke Press, 1994.

THE BEST HOT DOGS

TOOLS:

Cutting board
Knife
Mixing bowl
Can opener
Measuring spoons

Wooden spoon
Aluminum foil
Casserole dish
Tongs

INGREDIENTS:

1 small yellow onion
1 cup canned kidney beans
1 tablespoon prepared mustard
1 tablespoon brown sugar

$1/2$ tablespoon chili powder
2 strips bacon
6 beef hot dogs
6 hot dog buns

STEPS: MAKES 6

1 Place the onion on the cutting board. Carefully cut the ends off and discard. Cut the onion in half. Remove the skins and discard. Carefully cut the onion into $1/4$-inch cubes and place them into the mixing bowl.

2 Open the can of beans and place in the mixing bowl.

3 Add the mustard, brown sugar, and chili powder. Mix with the wooden spoon.

4 Place the bacon on the cutting board. Cut into $1/4$-inch pieces.

5 Cut 2 pieces of aluminum foil into 16-inch lengths. Place one piece of foil on top of the other.

6 Place the bacon in the center of the cut foil.

7 Spoon the ingredients of the mixing bowl onto the bacon. Make sure to keep all the ingredients in the center of the foil.

8 Place the hot dogs in the center. Carefully fold the foil toward the center to cover the hot dogs. Place them in the casserole dish.

9 Bake in a 375°F oven for 20 minutes.

10 Remove from oven and carefully open the foil. Using the tongs, remove the hot dogs and place each one in a hot dog bun. Spoon 2 tablespoons of the bean mixture over each hot dog and serve.

Note: You can cook this recipe on a barbecue grill if you wish. Place the foil-wrapped hot dogs on the grill and cook for 10 to 15 minutes.

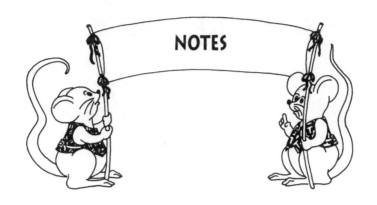

NOTES

CHAPTER 8

AUGUST

9   Roll out the other half of the pie dough on a clean, floured surface. Cover the top of the apples. Using a knife, carefully cut the top crust even with the pie pan.

10 Using clean fingers, pinch the top and bottom crusts together, moving around the crust until the pie is sealed.

11 Place the milk into the small glass bowl. Using the pastry brush, brush milk onto the top of the pie.

12 Sprinkle the 2 tablespoons of sugar over the crust.

13 Use the knife to cut six 2-inch slits into the top of the pie.
    Place the pie on a baking sheet. Put into a preheated, 375°F oven for 45 to 50 minutes.

Note: Serve warm with vanilla ice cream.

PIE CRUST

TOOLS:

Measuring cups
Mixing bowl
Measuring spoons
Fork

Small glass bowl
Cutting board (18 x 18 inches)
Knife
Rolling pin

INGREDIENTS:

2 cups flour
$^2/_3$ cup shortening
6 tablespoons cold water

1 teaspoon salt
$^1/_4$ cup flour

STEPS: MAKES 2 CRUSTS

1   Measure 2 cups flour into mixing bowl.

2   Divide shortening into 4 equal portions. Add 1 portion at a time to flour. Blend with a fork. When all shortening is blended it should have the consistency of cornmeal.

3   Place the cold water in the glass bowl. Add salt.

4   Using a tablespoon, add the cold water 1 drop at a time. Blend with the fork. For a flaky crust, do not overblend the ingredients.

5   When all the water is added, roll the dough into a ball. Cut in half. Adjust water as needed.

6   Place 1 piece of dough on a lightly floured board. Roll out to the desired size. For a two-crust pie, roll out the bottom crust slightly larger than the pie pan you are using.

7   Place the rolled dough into the bottom of the pie pan.

8   Fill with pie filling. Trim the crust even with the pie pan.

9   Roll out the other half of the dough. Place on top of pie filling. Trim the pie crust. Pinch with fingers to seal.

Note: If making a pie with only a bottom crust, wrap the remaining crust in plastic and refrigerate up to 1 week.

NOTES

CHAPTER 9

SEPTEMBER

LABOR DAY (FIRST MONDAY)

LABOR DAY

by Geoffrey Scott
(MINNEAPOLIS, MINN.: CAROLRHODA BOOKS, 1982)

Labor Day, a relatively young holiday, originated in New York City in the late 1800s. People worked long hours, sometimes seven days a week. With the forming of craft unions, people worked to change working conditions. Many created their own observations, but in 1882, 10,000 workers joined the first Labor Day parade.

SANDPAPER BLOCKS

MATERIALS:

2 blocks of wood, approximately
    4 x 3 x 1 inches
Coarse grade sandpaper
Pencil
Heavy duty scissors
Thumbtacks

DIRECTIONS:

Place the block of wood along the edge of a piece of sandpaper. Use the pencil to draw a line for cutting the other edge. The sandpaper should be long enough to wrap around the block. (Sandpaper does not need to overlap.) Cut the strip of sandpaper. Use the thumbtacks to hold the sandpaper in place. March in your own Labor Day parade, brushing the blocks in rhythm to marching music.

PICNIC CHEESE SPREAD

TOOLS:

Mixing bowl
Wooden spoon
Measuring cups

Measuring spoon
Plastic container with lid

INGREDIENTS:

6 ounces cream cheese, softened
12 ounces cheddar cheese, grated
$1/_2$ cup mayonnaise
1 tablespoon Dijon mustard

1 dash Worcestershire sauce
$1/_3$ cup chopped pimentos
Bread, crackers, or celery sticks

STEPS: SERVES 4–6

1 Place the cream cheese in the mixing bowl.

2 Stir the cream cheese with the wooden spoon. Slowly stir in the cheddar cheese.

3 Add the mayonnaise, mustard, and Worcestershire sauce. Blend with the wooden spoon.

4 Drain off the liquid from the pimentos and stir into the cheese spread.

5 Spoon the cheese spread into a plastic container and cover. Store in the refrigerator until ready to take on your picnic.

6 Use the spread to make a sandwich, to spread on crackers, or to fill celery sticks.

ROSH HASHANAH

(FIRST AND SECOND DAYS OF TISHRI ON THE JEWISH CALENDAR)

THE WORLD'S BIRTHDAY: A ROSH HASHANAH STORY

by Barbara Diamond Goldin
(SAN DIEGO: HARCOURT BRACE JOVANOVICH, 1990)

Daniel loved wearing new clothes for Rosh Hashanah, looking forward to the challahs, round, braided egg breads. After his father tells him the story of how Rosh Hashanah celebrates the world's first birthday, he decides to create a party for the world. Celebrate Rosh Hashanah by making a cake or have the traditional challahs in the following recipe.

ROSH HASHANAH CARD

MATERIALS:

9- x 12-inch sheet of construction
    paper
Scissors
2- x 3-inch sheet of construction
    paper
Markers or crayons
Glue

DIRECTIONS:

Fold the 9- x 12-inch sheet of construction paper in half. Crease the smaller piece of construction paper about $1/4$ inch from one edge. Place glue along this $1/4$-inch area. Glue the paper to the inside center of your folded card. You should be able to lift this piece of paper. Decorate by drawing leaves or another fall design on the outside of the card. Write a new year's message under the flap and decorate the inside of the card. Don't forget to sign the card with your name.

RELATED BOOKS

Yolen, Jane. *Milk and Honey: A Year of Jewish Holidays.* New York: G. P. Putnam's Sons, 1996.

Zalben, Jane Breskin. *Happy New Year, Beni.* New York: Henry Holt, 1993.

CHALLAH BREAD

TOOLS:

Measuring cups
Thermometer
1 large mixing bowl
Measuring spoons
Wooden spoon
Electric mixer

2 glass bowls
2 dishcloths
2 baking pans sheets
Pastry brush
Small glass bowl
Fork

INGREDIENTS:

2 cups warm water (100 to 110°F)
2 tablespoons active dry yeast
1 tablespoon sugar
$\frac{1}{3}$ cup vegetable oil
3 tablespoons honey
2 teaspoons salt

3 eggs
$7\frac{1}{2}$ cups flour
2 tablespoons vegetable oil
1 egg
Small glass bowl
1 tablespoon water

STEPS: MAKES 4 LOAVES

1   Place the water in the mixing bowl. Add the yeast and sugar. Mix with the wooden spoon and set aside for 10 minutes.

2   Add the vegetable oil, honey, and salt to the yeast water. Mix well with the wooden spoon.

3   Carefully crack 3 eggs into the mixture. Beat with mixer on low until blended.

4   Using the mixer, blend in 5 cups of flour, 1 cup at a time, to the mixture.

5   Using clean hands, gradually mix in 2 more cups of flour into the dough.

6   Sprinkle the remaining $\frac{1}{2}$ cup flour on a clean, dry surface. Place the dough on it and knead in the remaining flour. Continue to knead the dough for 10 minutes.

7   Separate the dough into two equal parts and place into 2 glass bowls. Cover with clean dishcloths. Let set at room temperature for $1\frac{1}{2}$ hours.

8   Remove the dough from the bowls. Separate into 6 equal parts. Roll each piece into 10- to 12-inch ropes. The ends of the rolled dough should be slightly thinner than the middles.

9 Place 3 pieces of dough next to each other and pinch the top ends together. Braid the three dough pieces by taking the piece on the right and bringing it over the middle piece. Then take the left piece and bring it over the middle piece. Continue to braid the dough until the three ends meet. Pinch them together. Repeat the braiding until there are 4 braided loaves.

10 Using a pastry brush, grease the baking sheets. Place the loaves onto them. Cover the loaves with 2 dish cloths. Let stand at room temperature for 30 minutes.

11 Carefully crack 1 egg into a small glass bowl. Add the tablespoon of water. Beat with the fork.

12 Remove dishcloths from the loaves. Gently brush loaves with the beaten egg mixture.

13 Place the loaves in a preheated 350°F oven. Bake for 35 to 45 minutes. Remove from oven. Let cool before slicing.

AMERICAN INDIAN DAY (FOURTH FRIDAY)

THIRTEEN MOONS ON TURTLE'S BACK: A NATIVE AMERICAN YEAR OF MOONS

by Joseph Bruchac and Jonathan London
(NEW YORK: PHILOMEL, 1992)

Many Native American cultures believe that the markings on a turtle's shell represent the thirteen moons of the year, each with its own story. Of the thirteen moons, several offer opportunities to celebrate foods of the Native Americans: maple sugar moon, strawberry moon, moon when acorns appear, and moon of wild rice. The moon stories are drawn from thirteen Native American tribal nations to provide variety to the stories.

RESEARCHING MAHNOMIN

DIRECTIONS:

Research the sacred food of the Ojibway people, *mahnomin*, which is a kind of water grass. Find out where rice is harvested by Native Americans and how other cultures use rice in their diets. Research favorite Native American foods such as corn. Begin your research with the books listed below and then sample some of the foods.

RELATED BOOKS

Braine, Susan. *Drumbeat … Heartbeat: A Celebration of the Powwow.* Minneapolis, Minn.: Lerner, 1995.

Caduto, Michael J., and Joseph Bruchac. *Native American Gardening: Stories, Projects and Recipes for Families.* Golden, Colo.: Fulcrum, 1996.

Hunter, Sally M. *Four Seasons of Corn.* Minneapolis, Minn.: Lerner, 1997.

Regguinti, Gordon. *The Sacred Harvest: Ojibway Wild Rice Gathering.* Minneapolis, Minn.: Lerner, 1992.

Wittsock, Laura Waterman. *Ininatig's Gift of Sugar: Traditional Native Sugarmaking.* Minneapolis, Minn.: Lerner, 1993.

WILD RICE

TOOLS:

Medium bowl

Measuring cups

Medium saucepan

Spoon

INGREDIENTS:

1 cup uncooked wild rice

$1/_2$ cup dried cranberries

$3^1/_2$ to 4 cups poultry or vegetable
  broth

Crumbled chestnuts, optional for
  topping

STEPS: SERVES 6-8

1 Place rice in bowl. Fill with cold water. Pour off water and repeat until
   rice is rinsed clean.

2 Place rice, cranberries, and $3^1/_2$ cups of broth in saucepan. Bring to a
   boil and simmer for 30 minutes, stirring occasionally.

3 Check rice. If it is still tough and all the broth is gone, add remaining
   broth and simmer for an additional 15 minutes.

4 Drain rice. Garnish with crumbled chestnuts, if desired.

Mouse at Work

CHAPTER 10

OCTOBER

COLUMBUS DAY (OCTOBER 12)

ALL PIGS ON DECK: CHRISTOPHER COLUMBUS'S SECOND MARVELOUS VOYAGE

by Laura Fischetto
(NEW YORK: DELACORTE PRESS, 1991)

When Columbus sets out on his second voyage to the Americas, he wants to take back seeds, farmers, carpenters, and other tradesmen. A man joins the ship with some pigs who make all sorts of trouble. Later they discover that the pigs were greatly appreciated.

EGG CARTON BOATS

MATERIALS:

Styrofoam egg carton
Scissors
Scraps of cloth or paper
Tape
Skewer

DIRECTIONS:

Cut the lid off the egg carton. Cut the portion that holds the eggs so that it is divided in the middle. (Cut it along the shortest portion.) Cut out a small sail. Tape to the top of the skewer. Shorten the skewer, if preferred. Insert the skewer through the lip of the carton. Float the boat in a sink of water. Experiment with adding weights in various places. Cut another boat by dividing between four and eight eggs. Compare those. Compare the small boats to what the top half of the carton can carry.

RELATED BOOKS

Roop, Peter, and Connie Roop, eds. *I, Columbus: My Journal—1492–3*. New York: Walker, 1990.

Sis, Peter. *Follow the Dream: The Story of Christopher Columbus*. New York: Alfred A. Knopf, 1991.

Smith, Barry. *The First Voyage of Christopher Columbus, 1492*. New York: Penguin, 1992.

BACON-WRAPPED DATES

TOOLS:

Plate   Fork
Paper towels   Scissors
Microwave oven   Toothpicks

INGREDIENTS:

10 slices bacon
20 dates

STEPS: MAKES 20

1 Place several paper towels on the plate.

2 Place three or four strips of bacon on the paper towels. Add a layer of paper towels. Repeat with the bacon, ending with a paper towel on top.

3 Cook on high for 6 minutes in the microwave oven. Check bacon. Cook 1 minute longer if bacon is nearly done, but do not let bacon become crisp. Loosen the bacon from the paper towels with the fork.

4 Quickly cut the bacon strips in half without letting the bacon cool.

5 Roll each bacon half around one date. Pierce with a toothpick to hold them together.

6 When all the dates are wrapped, arrange them on fresh paper towels on a plate. Microwave 1 to 2 minutes until bacon crisps a bit just before serving. Be careful not to overcook; the dates become much hotter than the bacon due to the high sugar content.

Note: You can replace the dates with water chestnuts.

HALLOWEEN (OCTOBER 31)

ARTHUR'S HALLOWEEN

by Marc Brown
(NEW YORK: TRUMPET CLUB, 1982)

Arthur finds Halloween entirely too overwhelming—the costumes, the gross treats, and the spooky decorations. When his little sister goes into the witch's house on the corner, he has to follow her. To his surprise he discovers a lovely old lady, Mrs. Tibble, who serves his favorite snack—chocolate doughnuts and apple cider.

HALLOWEEN FACE PAINTS

MATERIALS:

1 tablespoon shortening
2 tablespoons cornstarch
Food coloring
Small plastic storage containers

DIRECTIONS:

Mix together the shortening and cornstarch. Add a drop of food coloring of your choice and mix well. Store face paint in a container for five to seven days. Repeat the process with other colors or leave one batch white. Practice painting on your face before Halloween so you can create a special face that evening.

RELATED BOOKS

Andrews, Sylvia. *Rattlebone Rock*. New York: HarperCollins, 1995.
Barth, Edna. *Witches, Pumpkins, and Grinning Ghosts: The Story of the Halloween Symbols*. New York: Clarion Books, 1972.
Bunting, Eve. *The Haunted House*. New York: Trumpet Club, 1992.
Gillis, Jennifer. *In a Pumpkin Shell: Over 20 Pumpkin Projects for Kids*. Powal, Vt.: Storey Communications, 1992.
Williams, Linda. *The Little Old Lady Who Was Not Afraid of Anything*. New York: HarperCollins, 1986.

ARTHUR'S HALLOWEEN CIDER

TOOLS:

2-quart saucepan
Measuring cup
Wooden spoon

Plate
4 8-ounce mugs

INGREDIENTS:

1 quart apple cider
$\frac{1}{4}$ cup brown sugar

2 whole cloves
6 cinnamon sticks

STEPS: SERVES 6

1   Pour the apple cider into the saucepan and place on burner on low heat.

2   Carefully add the brown sugar. Stir with the wooden spoon.

3   Add the cloves and cinnamon sticks. Continue to simmer for 20 minutes, stirring every minute or so.

4   After 20 minutes, remove the cloves and cinnamon sticks with the wooden spoon. Discard cloves. Place cinnamon sticks on the plate.

5   Pour equal parts of the cider into 6 mugs. Place one cinnamon stick in each mug. Serve hot.

NOTES

CHAPTER 11

NOVEMBER

DAY OF THE DEAD (NOVEMBER 2)

MARIA MOLINA AND THE DAYS OF THE DEAD

by Kathleen Krull
(NEW YORK: MACMILLAN, 1994)

Maria enjoys every aspect of the Days of the Dead—even napping in a graveyard! She looks forward to next year's festivities, until her parents move to the United States to look for work. Soon she looks forward to celebrating Halloween in the United States, while still honoring her family. Try the recipe for Pan de los Muertos *in the book or the following recipe.*

GRAVESTONE RUBBINGS

MATERIALS:

Variety of plain paper such as newsprint, typing paper, and construction paper
Regular and colored pencils
Crayons

DIRECTIONS:

Go to a nearby graveyard. If the graveyard is attended, ask for permission to do some rubbings. Choose an interesting stone or marker. Lay the paper on the stone and turn your pencil or crayon flat. Rub across the marking. Lift and examine the effect. Try different pencils or crayons with different textures and compare the results.

RELATED BOOKS

Ancona, George. *Pablo Remembers.* New York: Lothrop, Lee and Shepard, 1993.
Erlbach, Arlene. *Soda Pop.* Minneapolis, Minn.: Lerner Publications, 1994.
Johnston, Tony. *Day of the Dead.* San Diego: Harcourt Brace, 1997.

CHOCOLATE SODA

TOOLS:

Measuring cups
4 10-ounce glasses

Measuring spoon
Spoon

INGREDIENTS:

1 cup chocolate syrup
4 tablespoons milk
2 cups soda water

$1\frac{1}{3}$ cups chocolate ice cream
Nutmeg

STEPS: SERVES 4

1   Place $\frac{1}{4}$ cup chocolate syrup into each glass.

2   Add 1 tablespoon milk to each glass.

3   Pour $\frac{1}{4}$ cup soda water into each glass. Stir with a spoon.

4   Pour $\frac{1}{4}$ cup more soda water into each glass.

5   Use the nutmeg container to sprinkle nutmeg on the tops of the drinks.

VETERANS DAY (NOVEMBER 11)

THE WALL

by Eve Bunting
(NEW YORK: CLARION BOOKS, 1990)

A young boy and his father visit the Vietnam Memorial in Washington, D.C. While finding the grandfather's name, the boy sees how others react to the names and mementos. After placing a school picture next to the part of the wall bearing his grandfather's name, the young boy leaves with his father, proud that his grandfather's name is on the wall, but wishing his grandfather was with him.

INTERVIEWING A VETERAN

DIRECTIONS:

Find out who in your family served in one of the armed forces. Arrange for an interview and ask the veterans various questions such as when they served, where they were stationed, which branch they belonged to, what they liked best about the military, what they wore, what they ate, and so forth. Ask to see photos and mementos of their experiences. If possible, use a tape recorder to preserve the interview.

RELATED BOOKS

Donnelly, Judy. *Wall of Names: The Story of the Vietnam Veterans Memorial*. New York: Random House, 1991.

Ransom, Candice F. *Jimmy Crack Corn*. Minneapolis, Minn.: Carolrhoda Books, 1994.

VICTORY GARDEN STUFFED PEPPERS

TOOLS:

Knife
Cutting board
Medium saucepan
Colander
Frying pan

Measuring cups
Measuring spoons
Wooden spoon
Deep baking dish

INGREDIENTS:

4 large green peppers
1 quart water
$\frac{1}{2}$ pound ground beef
1 small onion, chopped
1 cup cooked rice

$\frac{1}{2}$ cup drained canned tomatoes
1 tablespoon chopped parsley
$\frac{1}{2}$ teaspoon paprika
Salt and pepper to taste
1 cup water
Tomato sauce

STEPS: MAKES 4

1 Cut the tops off the peppers. Remove the seeds and membranes.

2 Place the peppers and tops in 1 quart boiling water for 10 minutes. Remove and drain upside down in a colander.

3 Sauté the ground beef and onion until the beef is brown and the onions are soft. Remove from heat.

4 Add rice, tomatoes, parsley, paprika, salt, and pepper. Mix with the wooden spoon.

5 Place the peppers in a deep baking dish. Place the beef mixture in the peppers. Place the lids on top.

6 Pour the water into the dish around the peppers. Bake in a preheated 350°F oven for 30 minutes. Add water if needed.

7 Serve the peppers with heated tomato sauce.

(Adapted from *Celebration of American Food: Four Centuries in the Melting Pot* by Gerry Schremp. Golden, Colo.: Fulcrum, 1996, page 82.)

THANKSGIVING (FOURTH THURSDAY)

GRACIAS THE THANKSGIVING TURKEY

by Joy Cowley
(NEW YORK: SCHOLASTIC PRESS, 1996)

Papá sends Miguel a turkey to raise for Thanksgiving. The turkey and Miguel become inseparable, with the turkey even following Miguel to church. Once the turkey is blessed by the priest, it becomes clear that the turkey cannot be Thanksgiving dinner. Chicken serves as the substitute and the turkey will have a new home at a petting zoo. (See Lorna Balian's Sometimes It's Turkey, Sometimes It's Feathers *for a similar story.)*

THANKSGIVING PLACEMATS

MATERIALS:

Large sheets of construction paper
Masking tape
Crayons, paints, markers

DIRECTIONS:

Divide the sheets of construction paper into four or six sections by folding the paper in half or thirds. Use the masking tape to divide the sections. Have each family member choose one or two sections to draw or paint something they are thankful for. Young children may simply paint or fill the section with color. Others may be more elaborate. Use the placemats for your Thanksgiving feast.

RELATED BOOKS

Balian, Lorna. *Sometimes It's Turkey, Sometimes It's Feathers.* Watertown, Wisc.: Humbug Books, 1994.

Brown, Marc. *Arthur's Thanksgiving.* Boston: Little, Brown, 1983.

Bunting, Eve. *How Many Days to America?: A Thanksgiving Story.* New York: Clarion, 1988.

Prelutsky, Jack. *It's Thanksgiving.* New York: Scholastic, 1982.

Mandrell, Louis, and Ace Collins. *Runaway Thanksgiving: A Story About the Meaning of Thanksgiving.* Fort Worth, Tex.: The Summit Group, 1992.

THANKSGIVING PUMPKIN MUFFINS

TOOLS:

Large mixing bowl
Electric mixer
Measuring cups
Small bowl

Measuring spoons
Pastry brush
3 12-muffin tins

INGREDIENTS:

29-ounce can pumpkin
3 eggs
4 cups sugar
1 cup peanut oil
5 cups unbleached white flour

1 tablespoon baking soda
1 tablespoon ground cinnamon
2 teaspoons ground cloves
$1\frac{1}{2}$ teaspoons salt
2 tablespoons melted butter

STEPS: MAKES 36

1 Place pumpkin, eggs, sugar, and peanut oil in a large mixing bowl. Mix with electric mixer.

2 Place flour in small bowl. Add baking soda, cinnamon, cloves, and salt.

3 Using electric mixer, blend flour mixture into pumpkin mixture.

4 Grease muffin tins with melted butter using a pastry brush.

5 Pour batter into tins, filling $^3/_4$ full.

6 Bake for 20 to 25 minutes in a preheated 350°F oven.

7 Remove from oven. Let cool. Remove muffins from tin.

Note: You may substitute safflower or canola oil for peanut oil. To make pumpkin bread loaves, divide batter between two 9- x 5- x 3-inch greased loaf pans and bake for approximately 1 hour at 350°F.

NOTES

Chapter 12

DECEMBER

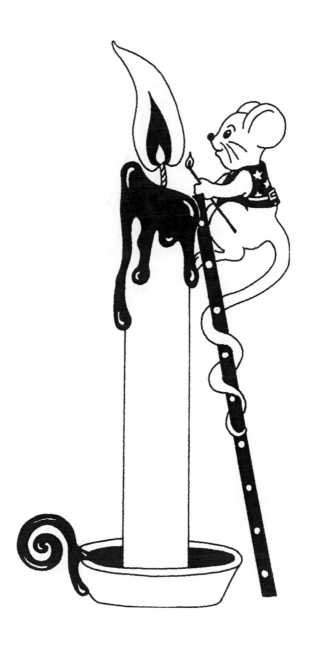

CHANUKKAH

(EIGHT DAYS, BEGINNING THE 25TH DAY OF KISLEV ON THE JEWISH CALENDAR)

THE CHANUKKAH GUEST

by Eric A. Kimmel
(NEW YORK: HOLIDAY HOUSE, 1988)

Because Bubba Brayna is ninety-seven years old and doesn't see or hear very well, she feeds a bear a huge feast of potato latkes, thinking he's the rabbi. When the rabbi and Bubba Brayna's friends arrive and realize her mistake, they all enjoy the thought of the bear having a very happy Chanukkah.

MENORAH

MATERIALS:

5- x 10- x 2-inch block of wood or Styrofoam
Markers, stars, ribbons, pretty paper, stickers, glitter
Ten nuts that will hold the candles
Glue
Scissors
Nine Hanukkah candles

DIRECTIONS:

Decorate the block of wood or Styrofoam with the markers and any materials you have available. Place nine nuts on the block of wood or Styrofoam so that they are evenly spaced. Glue in place. Add the tenth nut to the middle nut. Place the candles in the nuts.

RELATED BOOKS

Drucker, Malka. *Grandma's Latkes*. New York: Harcourt Brace Jovanovich, 1992.

Kimmel, Eric A. *Hershel and the Hanukkah Goblins*. New York: Holiday House, 1985.

———. *The Magic Dreidels: A Hanukkah Story*. New York: Holiday House, 1996.

Moss, Marissa. *The Ugly Menorah*. New York: Farrar Straus Giroux, 1996.

Yolen, Jane. *Milk and Honey: A Year of Jewish Holidays*. New York: G. P. Putnam's Sons, 1996.

Zalben, Jane Breskin. *Beni's First Chanukah*. New York: Henry Holt, 1988.

Note: Use with candles on pages 18–19.

POTATO LATKES

TOOLS:

Vegetable peeler
Vegetable grater
2-quart plastic bowl
Cutting board
Knife
Strainer
Mixing bowl

Measuring cups
Measuring spoons
Wire whip
Wooden spoon
Large heavy skillet (cast iron)
Slotted spatula
Baking sheet, lined with paper towels

INGREDIENTS:

3 russet potatoes
1 yellow onion
2 eggs
$1/3$ cup flour

1 tablespoon salt
$1/4$ teaspoon pepper
$1/2$ cup vegetable oil
Applesauce or sour cream

STEPS: MAKES 18–24

1   Using the vegetable peeler, remove and discard the skins from the potatoes.

2   Using the grater, grate the potatoes into the plastic bowl.

3   Place the onion onto the cutting board and carefully cut off and discard the ends. Cut the onion in half lengthwise. Remove and discard the skins.

4   Carefully grate the onion into the bowl with the potatoes.

5   Place the grated potato and onion into a strainer. Place the strainer on top of the mixing bowl. Using clean hands, gently press out the excess liquid from the potato and onion mixture. Return the mixture to the plastic bowl. Discard liquid.

6   Crack the eggs into the mixing bowl. Add the flour, salt, and pepper. Beat with the wire whip for 30 seconds.

7   Pour the egg mixture into the potato and onion mixture. Blend well with the wooden spoon.

8   Place the skillet on a burner on medium-high heat. Add the vegetable oil.

9 Carefully place 2 tablespoons of the potato mixture into the oil and gently press down the mixture with a wooden spoon. Place no more than 4 or 5 latkes into the oil at one time.

10 Cook the latkes for $1^1/_2$ minutes on one side. Carefully turn with the slotted spatula. Always turn the latkes away from your body.) Cook for 30 to 45 seconds longer.

11 Place the cooked latkes onto a baking sheet lined with paper towels. When all the latkes are cooked, place them onto a serving platter. Serve hot with applesauce or sour cream.

CHRISTMAS (DECEMBER 25)

AN AMISH CHRISTMAS

by Richard Ammon
(NEW YORK: ATHENEUM, 1996)

The children enjoy the school program in their one-room schoolhouse and all the last-minute preparations for Christmas. On the farm, they still have to help with the farm chores on Christmas Eve, but they manage to enjoy the cookie preparations. Finally they enjoy the simple exchange of gifts and the rich warmth of visiting with family and friends on Christmas Day.

SNOW PERSONS

MATERIALS:

1 cup flour
1 cup salt
1 cup water
Bowl
Spoon
Blue paper
Squeeze bottle such as a mustard
    container

DIRECTIONS:

Mix the flour, salt, and water in a bowl. Pour into a squeeze bottle. Squeeze onto blue paper in the shape of a snow person. The figure will puff up as it hardens. Experiment by adding facial features with raisins or spices.

RELATED BOOKS

Ahlberg, Janet, and Allan Ahlberg. *The Jolly Christmas Postman*. Boston: Little, Brown, 1991.

Bunting, Eve. *Going Home*. New York: HarperCollins, 1996.

Cushman, Doug. *Mouse and Mole and the Christmas Walk*. New York: W. H. Freeman, 1994.

Hegg, Tom. *A Cup of Christmas Tea*. Minneapolis, Minn.: Waldman House Press, 1982.

Rynbach, Iris Van. *Captain Cook's Christmas Pudding*. Honesdale, Pa.: Boyds Mill Press, 1997.

Sabuda, Robert. *The Christmas Alphabet*. New York: Orchard Books, 1994.

PEANUT CLUSTERS

TOOLS:

Double boiler
Measuring cup
Wooden spoon
Measuring spoon

Hot pad
2 cookie sheets
Waxed paper

INGREDIENTS:

2 cups water
1 pound semisweet chocolate

1 tablespoon light corn syrup
1 pound unsalted peanuts

STEPS: MAKES APPROXIMATELY 32

1   Place the water in the bottom of the double boiler. Place on medium heat.

2   Place the chocolate in the top portion of the double boiler. Place top portion on the bottom portion of the double boiler. Melt the chocolate, stirring occasionally with the wooden spoon.

3   Add the corn syrup to the chocolate. Stir with the wooden spoon.

4   Stir in the peanuts. Blend thoroughly.

5   Remove the double boiler from the burner. Place on a hot pad on the countertop.

6   Line the cookie sheets with waxed paper. Spoon out 1 tablespoon of the mixture until gone onto the cookie sheets. Let cool.

Note: If the chocolate hardens before you can make all the peanut clusters, return the double boiler to the burner and heat until the chocolate melts again.

KWANZAA (DECEMBER 26 TO JANUARY 1)

SEVEN CANDLES FOR KWANZAA

by Andrea Davis Pinkney
(NEW YORK: DIAL BOOKS, 1993)

Kwanzaa is like enjoying Thanksgiving, a birthday, and a day in the park. Beginning on December 26 and ending on January 1, it celebrates the first feasts of harvest with the holiday's seven principles. A book rich in colorful illustrations and text, it will make readers appreciate this American holiday inspired by African traditions.

BELL BRACELET

MATERIALS:

Five or six jingle bells
One or two thick pipe cleaners

DIRECTIONS:

Thread the jingle bells onto the pipe cleaner, spacing them evenly. Twist the ends of the pipe cleaner together and you have a bracelet or anklet. If the bells slip on the pipe cleaner, use two cleaners at once. This can be used as a gift, as a musical instrument, or for dancing.

RELATED BOOKS

Chocolate, Deborah M. Newton. *Kwanzaa.* Chicago: Children's Press, 1990.
Goss, Linda, and Clay Goss. *It's Kwanzaa Time.* New York: G. P. Putnam's Sons, 1995.
Hoyt-Goldsmith, Diane. *Celebrating Kwanzaa.* New York: Holiday House, 1993.
Porter, A. P. *Kwanzaa.* Minneapolis, Minn.: Carolrhoda Books, 1991.
Saint James, Cynthia. *The Gifts of Kwanzaa.* Morton Grove, Ill.: Albert Whitman, 1994.

BAKED SWEET POTATOES OR YAMS

TOOLS:

Vegetable peeler
Cutting board
Knife
2-quart casserole dish
Measuring cups

Measuring spoons
Mixing bowl
Wire whip
Aluminum foil

INGREDIENTS:

6 sweet potatoes or yams
$\frac{1}{2}$ cup apple juice
$\frac{1}{4}$ cup brown sugar
1 tablespoon cinnamon

$\frac{1}{2}$ teaspoon ground cloves
$\frac{1}{2}$ cup raisins
3 tablespoons butter

STEPS: SERVES 8-10

1   Using the vegetable peeler, carefully peel and discard the skins from the potatoes or yams.

2   Place the potatoes on the cutting board and cut them into half lengthwise.

3   Cut the lengths again into $\frac{1}{2}$-inch pieces.

4   Place the cut potatoes into the casserole dish.

5   Pour the apple juice into the mixing bowl. Add the brown sugar, cinnamon, and cloves. Blend with a wire whip for 30 seconds.

6   Pour the apple juice mixture onto the potatoes. Top with the raisins.

7   Place the butter onto the cutting board. Cut into small pieces and sprinkle them on top of the potatoes.

8   Cover the dish with aluminum foil. Place in a preheated 375°F oven and bake for 45 minutes. Carefully remove the foil and bake for an additional 10 to 15 minutes.

NEW YEAR'S EVE (DECEMBER 31)

DUMPLING SOUP

by Jama Kim Rattigan
(BOSTON: LITTLE, BROWN, 1993)

Marisa, a young Asian-American girl living in Hawaii, makes dumplings for the traditional New Year's Eve dumpling soup. She works with her Grandma, trying to do her best so her aunties will be impressed. Although the dumplings aren't as perfectly formed as those made by the more experienced members of the family, they taste wonderful and everyone celebrates her efforts.

NEW YEAR'S ROCKETS

MATERIALS:

Plastic drinking straw
Long balloon
Rubber band
3-inch square of paper
Pencil

DIRECTIONS:

Cut the straw in half. Fold or crimp the end of one straw half so that you can slip it into the other, creating a double straw. Slide the straw about half inch into the balloon. Use the rubber band to tightly wrap the balloon and straw together.

Fold the paper in half twice. Open it up. Place a dot with the pencil where the two folds meet. Push a small hole in the center with the pencil. Slip the straw through the hole.

Blow up the balloon through the straw, holding it by the rubber band. Let go and watch it fly. Experiment with size of balloons, placement of the paper fin, and amount of air. Happy New Year!

RELATED BOOKS

Edens, Cooper. *Santa Cow Island.* New York: Simon & Schuster, 1994.
Kalman, Bobbie, and Tina Holdcroft. *We Celebrate New Year.* New York: Crabtree Publishing, 1985.
Livingston, Myra Cohn. *New Year's Poems.* New York: Holiday House, 1987.
Model, Frank. *Goodbye Old Year, Hello New Year.* New York: Greenwillow Books, 1984.

DUMPLING SOUP

TOOLS:

Strainer
Measuring cups
Cutting board
Knife
Mixing Bowl
Wooden spoon

Measuring spoons
Fork
2-quart saucepan
Slotted spoon
4 soup bowls

INGREDIENTS FOR DUMPLINGS:

$1/_4$ cup water chestnuts
$1/_2$ pound ground pork
$1 1/_2$ teaspoons soy sauce
1 teaspoon sesame oil
$1 1/_2$ tablespoons cornstarch

$1/_4$ teaspoon salt
$1/_8$ teaspoon white pepper
16 dumpling wraps or wonton skins
1 quart water

STEPS: SERVES 4

1   Place the water chestnuts in a strainer and rinse under cold water for 30 seconds. Let drain.

2   Place the water chestnuts on the cutting board. Carefully cut into small pieces.

3   Place the chopped chestnuts into the mixing bowl. Add the ground pork. Mix well with the wooden spoon.

4   Add the soy sauce, sesame oil, corn starch, salt, and white pepper to the pork. Blend thoroughly.

5   Lay out the dumpling wraps on a clean, dry surface. Using the fork, place approximately 1 teaspoon of the mixture in the center of each wrap. Bring the corners of each dumpling wrap together. Gently squeeze the center to form a pocket of filling at the bottom with corners at the top. Make sure the dumplings are squeezed tight in the middle to keep the filling from coming out during cooking.

6   Place the water in the saucepan. Heat on medium high. When the water begins to boil, carefully place the dumplings into the pot using the slotted spoon. Cook the dumplings for 6 to 8 minutes.

7   When the dumplings are done, remove them with the slotted spoon. Place 4 dumplings in each soup bowl and set aside.

INGREDIENTS FOR BROTH:

4 cups canned chicken broth
1 tablespoon soy sauce
1 teaspoon sesame oil
$1/4$ teaspoon white pepper
2 green onion sprigs

STEPS:

1   Place the chicken broth in a saucepan. Heat on medium high.

2   Add the soy sauce, sesame oil, and white pepper. Stir with the wooden spoon.

3   Place the green onions on the cutting board. Carefully cut off the ends and discard. Cut the onions into $1/4$-inch pieces and set aside.

4   When the broth begins to boil, carefully remove it from the stove. Add 8 ounces to each of the soup bowls containing the dumplings.

5   Garnish the soup with the chopped green onion. Serve immediately.

NOTES

CHAPTER 13

GENERAL

BIRTHDAY PARTY

HAPPY BIRTHDAY, DEAR DUCK

by Eve Bunting
(NEW YORK: CLARION BOOKS, 1988)

Duck, who lives in the desert, is puzzled by birthday gifts from his friends: a swimming suit, wide-brimmed hat, floating chair, fishing rod, and various water toys. Finally turtle arrives with the gift that makes everything appropriate: a large plastic pool. After they all enjoy a swim, they enjoy a feast of corn crackle cakes, grasshopper cookies, and polliwog shakes.

BIRTHDAY PARTY FAVORS

MATERIALS:

Toilet paper tubes
Markers
Construction paper
Scissors
Pencil
Tape
Squares of tissue paper
Small gifts: marbles, jacks, rings, cars
Candies (optional)

DIRECTIONS:

Use the markers and construction paper to decorate the toilet paper tubes. Place each tube upright on a small piece of construction paper. Trace around the circle. Cut the circle out and tape it to one end of the tube. Fill the tube with the small gifts or candies. Loosely crumple the tissue paper and place it in the other end of the tube. Decorate the table with the favors. This activity may be used for other holidays.

RELATED BOOKS

Bridwell, Normal. *Clifford's Birthday Party.* New York: Scholastic, 1988.
Brown, Marc. *Arthur's Birthday Party.* Boston: Little, Brown, 1989.
Bunting, Eve. *The Wednesday Surprise.* New York: Clarion Books, 1989.
Haas, Irene. *A Summertime Song.* New York: Simon & Schuster, 1997.
Holabird, Katharine. *Angelina's Birthday Surprise.* New York: Clarkson N. Potter, 1989.
Ichikawa, Satomi. *Happy Birthday! A Book of Birthday Celebrations.* New York: Philomel, 1988.

GRASSHOPPER COOKIES

TOOLS:

2 cookie sheets
Measuring spoons
2 1-quart mixing bowls
Fork

Measuring cups
Cutting board
Knife

INGREDIENTS:

8 slices white bread
$1/_4$ teaspoon green food coloring
2 tablespoons water

$1^1/_2$ cups flake coconut
2 cups sweetened condensed milk

STEPS: MAKES 8-16 COOKIES

1   Place the bread slices on the cookie sheets. Let stand at room
    temperature for 1 hour.

2   Place the green food coloring into one of the mixing bowls. Add the 2
    tablespoons of water. Mix with the fork.

3   Carefully add the coconut. Mix with the fork and set aside.

4   Place the bread on a cutting board. Cut into grasshopper shapes.

5   Place the sweetened condensed milk into the other mixing bowl. Using
    clean hands, dip the bread pieces into the milk. Then dip into the
    colored coconut. Place the dipped bread onto a cookie sheet.

6   Bake in a preheated 350°F oven for 8 to 10 minutes.

7   Let cool for at least 20 minutes.

TEA PARTY

MISS SPIDER'S TEA PARTY

by David Kirk
(NEW YORK: SCHOLASTIC, 1994)

Miss Spider wishes the nearby insects would join her for tea. Afraid of being her next meal, the beetles, fireflies, bumblebees, ants, butterflies, and moths turn down her invitation. Finally, one wet moth asks for shelter, discovering Miss Spider means no harm. The word spreads, and soon Miss Spider has many guests for tea.

RELATED BOOKS

Carle, Eric. *Do You Want to Be My Friend?* New York: Crowell, 1971.

———. *The Very Busy Spider*. New York: Philomel Books, 1985.

Durant, Alan. *Mouse Party*. Cambridge, Mass.: Candlewick Press, 1995.

104

STRAWBERRY SPIDER WEB PLATES

SPIDER SAUCE

TOOLS:

Measuring cups
Blender
Saucepan
Wooden spoon

Measuring spoon
Small mixing bowl
Strainer
Large mixing bowl

INGREDIENTS:

6 cups frozen strawberries, thawed
$1^1/_2$ cups sugar

$1^1/_4$ cups water
2 tablespoons cornstarch

STEPS:

1   Place thawed strawberries in blender no more than $^3/_4$ full. Hold lid on tightly. Blend on medium-high speed for 30 seconds. Place blended strawberries in saucepan. Repeat until all strawberries are blended.

2   Add sugar and 1 cup water to strawberries in saucepan. Cook over medium heat for 10 minutes. Stir with the wooden spoon every 30 seconds.

3   Mix cornstarch with remaining water in small mixing bowl. Add to hot strawberry sauce. Stir with the wooden spoon for 1 minute over low heat.

4   Remove mixture from heat. Let stand for 2 minutes.

5   Place strainer over large mixing bowl. Carefully pour sauce through strainer. Use wooden spoon to stir the sauce and push mixture through the strainer.

6   Set sauce aside until ready to use.

SPIDER WEBBING

TOOLS:

Measuring cups
Mixing bowl
Wire whip

Squeeze bottle (empty, clean mustard or
    honey bottle)

INGREDIENTS:

2 cups sour cream
$\frac{1}{4}$ cup half-and-half

STEPS:

1 Place sour cream in mixing bowl. Whip with wire whip.

2 Mix sour cream slowly and add half-and-half.

3 Put sour cream mixture into squeeze bottle.

Note: May substitute plain yogurt for sour cream and half-and-half. However, plain yogurt is not as stable as the sour cream.

SPIDER WEB PLATE

TOOLS AND INGREDIENTS:

2-ounce ladle
Spider Sauce (see recipe on page 105)
Measuring spoon
24 8-inch plates

Spider Webbing
Squeeze bottle with Spider Webbing
   (see recipe on page 106)
Toothpicks

STEPS: MAKES 24 PLATES

1   Using ladle, pour 4 tablespoons of sauce onto each plate. Move plate from side to side until sauce covers entire surface. Do not get sauce on rim of plate.

2   Using squeeze bottle, draw a spiral shape from the center to the outside edge. Lines should be about 1 inch apart.

3   Using a toothpick, start in the center of the plate and drag the toothpick lightly to the outside edge. Repeat every $^1/_4$ inch until the spider web is formed.

4   Place spider muffin cake (see recipe on page 108) or other dessert in middle of web. Garnish with strawberries if desired.

Note: Spider web plates can be prepared ahead and chilled in the refrigerator for 1 day. (Do not stack plates.) Do not substitute yogurt for the sour cream and half-and-half mixture if preparing ahead.

SPIDER MUFFIN CAKES

TOOLS:

Double boiler
Measuring spoons
Measuring cups
2 mixing bowls
Wooden spoon

Fork
Electric mixer
Rubber spatula
Pastry brush
Muffin tin

INGREDIENTS:

4 tablespoons butter
3 ounces unsweetened chocolate
$1\frac{3}{4}$ cups flour
$1\frac{1}{3}$ cups sugar
$1\frac{1}{4}$ teaspoons baking powder
$\frac{1}{2}$ teaspoon baking soda

$\frac{1}{2}$ teaspoon salt
2 eggs
1 cup milk
$\frac{1}{2}$ teaspoon vanilla
$\frac{1}{2}$ cup chopped nuts
2 tablespoons melted butter

STEPS: MAKES 18

1   Place water in the bottom of a double boiler. Heat butter and chocolate in the top of the double boiler. Remove from heat when melted and set aside.

2   Place flour, sugar, baking power, baking soda, and salt in a large mixing bowl. Mix together with the spoon.

3   Crack the eggs into a separate bowl. Add the milk and vanilla. Beat with the fork until blended.

4   Use the electric mixer to blend the milk mixture into the flour. Beat on low speed for 30 seconds.

5   Add the melted butter and chocolate to the mixture. Use the rubber spatula to scrape the chocolate out of the top of the double boiler.

6   Beat the mixture on medium for 2 minutes.

7   Scrape the blades of the mixture with the rubber spatula into the bowl. Add the chopped nuts. Mix with the wooden spoon.

8   Use the pastry brush to lightly grease the muffin tin with the melted butter.

9   Fill each muffin cup $\frac{3}{4}$ full. Place in a preheated 350°F oven. Bake for 15 to 20 minutes. To test cake for doneness, insert a clean toothpick into the center of the cake. If the toothpick is sticky, return the muffin tin to the oven for a few more minutes.

APPENDIX A:
HIGH-ALTITUDE ADJUSTMENTS

BREADS

Reduce the baking soda or baking powder by one-fourth.

CAKES

At high elevations up to 3,000 feet:
Raise the baking temperature about 25°F.
Underbeat the eggs.

At high elevations above 3,000 feet:
Raise the baking temperature about 25°F.
Underbeat the eggs.
Reduce the baking powder or baking soda by about $1/_8$ teaspoon for each teaspoon called for in the recipe.

At 5,000 feet:
Raise the baking temperature about 25°F.
Underbeat the eggs.
Reduce the baking powder or baking soda by about $1/_2$ teaspoon for each teaspoon called for in the recipe.
Decrease sugar 1 to 2 tablespoons for each cup.
Increase liquid 1 to 2 tablespoons for each cup.

For all high altitudes:
Grease and flour all baking pans well. Cakes tend to stick.

CANDY

For each increase of 500 feet above sea level, cook candy syrups 1°F lower than indicated in the recipes.

WATER

Boiling temperatures:

Sea level	212°F
2,000 feet	208°F
5,000 feet	203°F
7,500 feet	198°F

APPENDIX B:
MEASURING ACCURATELY

Flour: Dip measuring cup into flour. Level off extra with a knife.

Sugar (granulated or confectioner's): Spoon into a measuring cup. Level off with a knife.

Brown sugar: Pack brown sugar into a measuring cup. It should hold its shape when turned out of the cup.

Shortening: Use spatula or scraper to pack it into a measuring cup. Level off with a knife.

Liquids: Pour into cup. A glass liquid measuring cup allows extra room at the top, preventing spilling. Molasses and syrup "round" up, so pour slowly. Use a spatula or rubber scraper to scrape out cup.

Nuts, coconut, bread crumbs, cheese: Pack measuring cup lightly until full.

Spices, baking powder, salt: Fill measuring spoon and level off with a knife.

MEASURING EQUIVALENTS

Dash = less than $1/8$ teaspoon

3 teaspoons = 1 tablespoon

4 tablespoons = $1/4$ cup

$5 1/3$ tablespoons = $1/3$ cup

8 tablespoons = $1/2$ cup

$10 2/3$ tablespoons = $2/3$ cup

12 tablespoons = $3/4$ cup

16 tablespoons = 1 cup

1 cup = $1/2$ pint

2 cups = 1 pint

2 pints (4 cups) = 1 quart

BUTTER OR MARGARINE

4 sticks = 1 pound = 2 cups

1 stick = $1/4$ pound = $1/2$ cup

$1/2$ stick = $1/8$ pound = $1/4$ cup

$1/8$ stick = 1 tablespoon

EGGS

Whole Medium	Whites	Yolks
1 = $1/4$ cup	2 = $1/4$ cup	3 = $1/4$ cup
2 = $1/3$ to $1/2$ cup	3 = $3/8$ cup	4 = $1/3$ cup
3 = $1/2$ to $2/3$ cup	4 = $1/2$ cup	5 = $3/8$ cup
4 = $2/3$ to 1 cup	5 = $2/3$ cup	6 = $1/2$ cup

GLOSSARY OF COOKING TERMS

Bake: to cook in an oven.

Beat: to mix with vigorous over-and-under motion with spoon, whip, or beater.

Blend: to mix thoroughly.

Boil: to cook liquid until bubbles break on the surface.

Brown: to bake or fry until brown in color.

Chill: to allow to become thoroughly cold, usually by placing in a refrigerator.

Chop: to cut in fine or coarse pieces with a knife.

Coat: to cover with thin film, such as with flour, crumbs, or sugar.

Cool: to allow to cool to room temperature.

Core: to remove the core of a fruit.

Crack: to break an egg by tapping the side of the egg on the edge of a bowl.

Cut in: to mix fat into flour using a pastry blender, fork, or two knives.

Dice: to cut into small (about $1/4$-inch) cubes.

Dissolve: to stir granules into a liquid until the granules are no longer visible.

Dot: to place small chunks of butter in several places on the top of ingredients.

Frost: to cover with icing.

Fry: to fry in a pan in shortening or oil.

Grate: to reduce to small particles by rubbing against a grater.

Knead: to work dough by pressing, folding, and stretching with the hands.

Mash: to mix or crush to a soft form.

Mix: to combine ingredients by stirring.

Peel: to remove the outside skin.

Pit: to remove pits or seeds from fruit.

Preheat: to turn on an oven or griddle in advance, so that it is at the correct temperature for baking or frying.

Rinse: to wash lightly, usually with water.

Roll: to place on a board and spread thin with a rolling pin.

Sauté: to cook or fry in a small amount of oil, shortening, or butter in a skillet.

Sift: to pass through a sieve to remove lumps.

Simmer: to cook in liquid just below the boiling point.

Skewer: to place chunks of food on a long metal or wooden spear for cooking.

Slice: to cut a thin, flat piece off.

Soak: to immerse in liquid.

Stir: to mix with a spoon.

Strain: to remove excess liquid, perhaps with a strainer or sieve.

Toss: to lightly mix ingredients.

Whip: to beat rapidly to incorporate air into the batter.

BIBLIOGRAPHY

Gustafson, Scott. *Alphabet Soup: A Feast of Letters*. Shelton, Conn.: The Greenwich Workshop Press, 1994.

Hoberman, Mary Ann. *The Seven Silly Eaters*. San Diego: Harcourt Brace, 1997.

Johnson, Sylvia A. *Tomatoes, Potatoes, Corn, and Beans: How the Foods of the Americas Changed Eating Around the World*. New York: Atheneum, 1997.

Leedy, Loreen. *The Edible Pyramid*. New York: Holiday House, 1994.

Livingston, Myra Cohn. *Celebrations*. New York: Holiday House, 1985.

Munsterberg, Peggy. *Beastly Banquet: Animal Poems*. New York: Dial Books, 1997.

Penner, Lucille Recht. *Celebration: The Story of American Holidays*. New York: Macmillan, 1993.

Rosen, Michael J. *Food Fight: Poets Join the Fight Against Hunger with Poems to Favorite Food*. San Diego: Harcourt Brace, 1996.

Thomas, Joyce Carol. *Gingerbread Days*. New York: HarperCollins, 1995.

Zamorano, Ana. *Let's Eat!* New York: Scholastic, 1996.

INDEX

ACTIVITIES AND TITLES

HOLIDAYS

Printed in the United States
133958LV00001B/1-10/A

9 781555 919726